The
GARDENER'S
POCKET BIBLE

The GARDENER'S POCKET BIBLE

EVERY GARDENING RULE OF THUMB
at your fingertips

RONI JAY

Editor Richard Craze
Consultant editors Jill Jay, Will Jones

new tricks for old dogs

Published by White Ladder Press Ltd
Great Ambrook, Near Ipplepen, Devon TQ12 5UL
01803 813343
www.whiteladderpress.com

First published in Great Britain in 2005

10 9 8 7 6 5 4 3

© Roni Jay 2005

The right of Roni Jay to be identified as author of this work has been
asserted by her in accordance with the Copyright, Designs and Patents
Act 1988.

ISBN 0 9548219 6 3

British Library Cataloguing in Publication Data
A CIP record for this book can be obtained from the British Library.

Designed and typeset by Julie Martin Ltd
Cover design by Julie Martin Ltd
Cover photographs by Jonathon Bosley
Illustration by Chris Mutter
Cover printed by St Austell Printing Company
Printed and bound by TJ International Ltd, Padstow, Cornwall

White Ladder Press
Great Ambrook, Near Ipplepen, Devon TQ12 5UL
01803 813343
www.whiteladderpress.com

Acknowledgements

I would like to thank my mother, Jill, who generously gave up an enormous amount of time to do the research for this book for me at short notice. She had the advantage of knowing pretty well all of the information already, so the research was largely a matter of double-checking her extensive knowledge in her arguably even more extensive library of gardening books. Nevertheless I can't thank her enough for all the effort she put in for me and for the book. And while I'm about it, I want to thank her for giving me my enthusiasm for gardening, and for all the work she's put into my gardens over the years.

She was helped enormously in her research by my father, Tony (this is a real family effort, as you can see), who supported her, read the manuscript, occasionally corrected her Latin spellings, and battled with a failing fax machine to send amendments and queries back and forth. Their friend Will, a professional gardener, spent hours on the phone and at the kitchen table with them both, filling in details and discussing the finer points of lawn care or root cuttings. I am deeply grateful to both of them too.

I would also like to thank Laurie Taylor for casting his professional eye over the manuscript and making sure that we hadn't made any glaring mistakes. I feel much happier for knowing that two professional gardeners have added their knowledge to my mother's huge practical experience and my own.

Finally, I would like to thank James Belsey for the enthusiasm and work that he put in to making this book as useful and as interesting as possible.

Contents

WILDLIFE GARDENING ∾

Introduction

How often have you found yourself happily working away in your garden, enjoying the relaxing fresh air and that therapeutic way your mind can drift aimlessly as you dig or plant or weed? And then you realise there's some garden job you need to do and can't quite remember how. Should you put this on the compost or the bonfire pile? How many buds are you supposed to leave when you prune this climbing rose? Should you cut these raspberry canes down now?

Suddenly, your relaxing afternoon in the garden turns into a frustrating choice between leaving the job undone, risking getting it wrong, or going indoors to look up the answer (where you know you'll get sidetracked).

Not any more. The idea for this book came from just such irritating moments. I've been gardening for several years, and I know a lot more about it than I once did. When I first started I used to phone my mother regularly and say, "I know you told me last year which clematis to cut right down to the ground, but I've forgotten again." I'm lucky to have a mother who has spent every spare minute gardening for the last 45 years and there's not much she doesn't know. Even so, it was frustrating to have to put down the secateurs and trudge off to the phone.

"What I need," I thought, "Is a quick reference guide I can take out into the garden with me to look up all those things on the spot." So this book is intended as the 'phone a friend' for anyone who doesn't have an expert gardener in the family, or who simply doesn't want to traipse indoors and phone them in the hope they're in.

∾ Using this book ∾

There are a few points I'd like to make about using this book. The information it contains is often specific, but in other cases I've given rules of thumb, as the subtitle indicates. The whole point about rules of thumb is that they almost always apply, but if you think you're dealing with one of the rare exceptions I'd advise you to double-check with a specialist source. You'll find that the experts frequently disagree on things like planting distances for vegetables, or whether it's OK to prune roses with a hedge trimmer. So rules of thumb are often about the best you'll get anyway.

Obviously the same answer doesn't always fit gardens from Cornwall to Orkney, or apply in exceptionally mild springs as well as very cold ones. Where it's possible I've pointed out variations. But gardeners are intelligent people with plenty of common sense, and I figure you can work out for yourself when you need to make allowances.

I find books which refer to every plant twice, once in Latin and once in English, very hard to read. So I haven't done it. I've used whichever version seems to be in most common usage, and I've then included an appendix at the back which gives all the plant names I've used. I've given English/Latin and Latin/English translations. You'll also find a comprehensive index at the back to help you find whatever you need to know.

I'm confident that you'll find this book immensely useful.

It is a personal collection of rules and guidance, though the information is factual and as thorough as I could manage. As a result you may find a slightly idiosyncratic approach to the use of imperial/metric measurements and the like, and you'll also find a bias in favour of organic and environmentally friendly gardening, without getting silly about it.

Please let me know if you feel anything important has been omitted, so I can include it in future editions. You can contact me on **roni@whiteladderpress.com**. In the meantime, I hope this book gives you the opportunity to spend even more of your time outside. Happy gardening.

Gardener's glossary

Gardening is one of those occupations which is over-grown with jargon. If you're serious as a gardener you won't get away with using simple words like dig, plant and weed. Oh, no. Plant enthusiasts practise a whole vocabulary of strange activities, some of which you hardly like to ask about, from top dressing to pricking out, hardening off and bedding out.

So that you can translate the backs of seed packets and the pages of gardening guides, here's a glossary of the most common gardening terms you'll find in this book and else-where. (We have tried not to insult your intelligence by defining terms such as flower, or spade.)

Acid soil	Soil with pH content below 7 (good for eg *heather, rhododendron, gentian*)
Activator	In composting, an ingredient which stimulates and accelerates the composting process (unfortunately there isn't yet an ingredient which stimulates and accelerates the gardener to get on with the less appealing garden jobs)
Alkaline soil	Soil with pH content above 7 (good for eg *clematis, poppy, fuchsia*)

Alpine	Plant which, in the wild, grows between the treeline and the snowline so hardy and usually small
Annual	A plant that lives for one year only
Bedding plant	A plant used for mass planting of the same type for instant display such as in parks, roundabouts etc (not one grown to stuff mattresses with)
Biennial	A plant that flowers only in its second year and dies after flowering. Some plants are not true biennials but are grown as such eg *wallflower, forget-me-not, sweet William*
Brassica	Member of the large cruciferae family of vegetables including *cabbages, cauliflower, Brussels sprouts, broccoli, kale*
Chit	Encouraging tubers such as *potatoes* to sprout before planting by exposing them to maximum daylight somewhere cool but frost free
Compost	Has two meanings: *a)* a mixture of different soils and nutrients *b)* rotted vegetable matter or farmyard manure
Cordon	Way of pruning that restricts a plant to a single main stem
Corm	A swollen stem base below the ground which stores food reserves. Unlike a

	bulb it isn't layered, but the whole is covered in papery scales
Cuttings	Sections of plants that are removed and used for propagation
Deadhead	Removing dead flower heads to prevent seeding and encourage further flowering
Disbud	Removing over-prolific buds to encourage fewer but larger flowers or fruit
Divide	A means of propagation in which you carefully separate the roots into two or more plants for replanting
Earth up	Piling up soil round plants to protect against frost (eg *potatoes*) or whiten the stem (eg *celery*)
Espalier	(From the French for 'shoulder') Training a tree to have a straight trunk and pairs of opposite branches running horizontally (often fruit trees against a wall)
Fan train	Pruning a tree or shrub so that the main branches fan out against a wall or a fence
Graft	Propagating by uniting the stem or bud of one plant with the root stock of another (or just good hard work, of course, which there's plenty of in the garden)

Half-hardy	(no relation to half-Nelson) Refers to two types of plant:
	a) frost-tender annuals planted out around the end of May for one summer only (eg *lobelia, African marigold*)
	b) shrubs and herbaceous perennials that need protection in winter (except in sheltered positions in mild areas)
Half ripe cuttings	Cuttings which are mainly green but include some woody material
Harden off	Gradually acclimatising plants that have been grown inside to the outside before planting out
Hardy	Frost-resistant, so can be grown outside all year round
Heel in	Temporary planting of bare-rooted plants until time or space are available for final planting
Herbaceous	A plant that dies down in winter but will come up again in spring
Humus	Partially decomposed organic matter in the soil which improves fertility and water retention. Don't be tempted to dip raw peeled vegetables in it and then eat them without first spelling it differently.
Invasive	Tough plants that will take over the whole garden if you don't watch them, either by spreading or by seeding (often

	used euphemistically in plant descriptions – it really means 'watch out')
Lateral	A side shoot from the stem of a plant
Layering	Propagate by pegging stem down to soil while it's still attached to parent plant, to root and create a new plant (eg *clematis*)
Loam	A reasonably fertile soil with a good balance of clay and sand particles and a high humus content. Loams are the most easily cultivated of all soil types and hold water and nutrients well.
Mulch	A layer of organic or inorganic matter spread on the surface around plants to protect roots from frost, conserve moisture, enrich soil and suppress weed growth (also a verb, 'to mulch' a plant)
Naturalise	To establish and grow as if in the wild
Neutral soil	soil with a pH balance of 7, the point at which soil is neither acid nor alkaline
Nursery bed	Area of the garden for rearing young plants before planting them out, and other temporary uses such as heeling in
Perennial	A plant that lives for more than two years

pH	A scale for measuring the acid/alkaline balance of soil, which affects what will happily grow in it
Pinch out	Removing certain growing points of a plant to promote bushiness (so not as mean as it sounds)
Pollination	Transferring pollen from one flower to another for fertilisation
Potting on	Moving from a smaller container to a larger one
Prick out	First planting out of seedlings or cuttings
Propagate	Increase the number of plants by seeding, cuttings, grafting etc
Prune	Cut back plant to restrict size, improve shape, or increase flowering or fruiting
Rhizome	Underground creeping stem that acts as a storage unit, similar to a bulb, in plants such as *iris* or *anemone nemorosa*
Rootstock	A well rooted plant base on which a scion is grafted; or the stock on to which a shoot of another similar plant is grafted
Runner	Aerial shoot that roots when it touches the ground and forms a separate plant, eg *strawberry*
Split	See *Divide*

Successional planting	Planting the same plants or seeds at time intervals (fortnight, 3 weeks or a month usually) to produce crops over a longer time period
Succulent	Having thick fleshy leaves (eg *house leek*) developed by plants in dry climates for water storage
Sucker	Shoot that comes direct from root or rootstock
Taproot	Main downgrowing and anchoring root eg *parsnip*
Tender	Liable to damage by frost
Thin out	Reducing the number of plants growing in a pot, tray, flower bed, vegetable garden etc by pulling some out to make more space available and reduce competition
Top dressing	Has two meanings: *a)* Removing top inch or two of soil and replacing with compost or fresh soil (almost always containers) *b)* Applying a layer of fertiliser to flower beds (eg *roses*) or lawns and vegetable gardens
Tuber	Thickened fleshy root (eg *dahlia*) or underground stem (eg *potato*) which acts as a storage organ
Woody	With a stem composed of woody fibres so the plant doesn't die right back to the ground in winter (eg *lavender*)

Frost facts

In some ways it must be a luxury gardening in warmer climates where you don't have to worry about frost. Then again, you wouldn't get the variety you do here. Certainly frost – or simply the threat of it – is a looming presence over British gardeners and controls much of what we can and can't grow.

Then again, frost does have its good points. It helps break down the soil, kills many dormant pests and diseases, and stimulates some seeds and bulbs to germinate.

Pocket facts

There is a difference between an air frost – where the temperature of the air itself drops below freezing – and a ground frost which is not so cold, as only the surface of the ground is affected where the dew freezes. This happens because cold air falls at night and accumulates at low points at ground level. Since the air isn't freezing, foliage isn't affected. Many tender plants, though by no means all, can resist a ground frost; it's the air frost that gets them. Even tender plants need only modest protection from ground frost.

The critical thing is not to expose any vulnerable plants to frost by mistake as you will very likely lose them. So the question right now is, can you safely plant out tender seedlings or leave out tender plants without danger of frost?

∽ Spring frosts ∽

Needless to say, there is no nice, convenient, helpful, clear answer to this. This is especially true lately as climate change seems to be taking effect. But there are clues to help you decide when the risk has passed. The most significant factor is where in the UK your garden is.

Spring, and the accompanying reduction in frost risk, moves up the country from south west to north east. It takes around eight weeks to travel from Cornwall to Orkney, which means it travels at about a third of a mile an hour. Here's a rough guide to the most likely last time for an air frost (ground frosts might occur later) in different parts of the UK (but no promises):

Plymouth	mid April
Bristol	mid April
Cardiff	late April
London	early May
Cambridge	early May
Birmingham	late May
Liverpool	early April
Leeds	early May
Edinburgh	early May
Isle of Skye	early April
Wick	late May

However you need to take other factors into account too, especially distance from the sea and height:

o You're more likely to get a late frost the further inland you are.

o Spring takes longer to reach higher ground – approx two days for every 100ft rise in height.

o Dry, light soil freezes more readily than damp soil and is therefore a risk for longer.

o Frost pockets can form in odd places. Cold air flows downhill like water into valleys or dips in the ground so a valley can be frostier than the hillside above.

So ideally, to minimise the risk of a late frost, you want to garden on low ground (but without any frost pockets) on the south west coast with naturally damp soil.

A word about frost pockets: if you've noticed that part of your garden is vulnerable to 'collecting' frost, you may be able to move a barrier out of the way to allow the cold air to flow through and escape. Simply replacing a solid fence with an open trellis, for example, can eliminate a frost pocket. There's a job for the weekend.

Rule of thumb

For every 250 feet above sea level, the temperature drops one degree Fahrenheit.

So what are you going to do about protecting those plants from an unexpected late frost? When it comes to hardy plants, not a lot – they'll be fine anyway. But some plants can be killed by frost early in the year (see below) and should be kept indoors, or in a frost free greenhouse, until any danger of frost has passed.

❧ Which plants are vulnerable in spring?

Flowering plants which are vulnerable to spring frosts include:

African marigold	fuchsia
ageratum	helichrysum petiolare
alyssum	heliotrope
argyranthemum	nemesia
begonia	pelargonium (geranium)
calceolaria	petunia
chocolate cosmos	salvia
cleome spinosa	snapdragon
felicia	tobacco plant

Fruit, vegetables and herbs which are susceptible include:

basil	marrow	squash
endive	pepper	sweetcorn
courgette	pumpkin	tomato
French beans	runner beans	

You can sow *runner beans* and *French beans* directly into the soil a couple of weeks before the last threat of frost so that their shoots don't appear above ground until the danger is past. You can also plant *potatoes, celery* and *chicory* earlier but earth them up to cover and protect the shoots until after the last frosts.

And one more thing to bear in mind before you summon up the courage to plant out your seedlings and move the *geraniums* back outside: even without a frost, cold winds can kill tender plants. So if you're in an exposed and windy area (such as the top of a hill, or almost anywhere in East Anglia) you may want to wait a little longer even when the frost risk has passed.

Suppose you've been caught out. You've planted out your summer bedding, or your potatoes are up, and now they tell you they're forecasting a late frost. Your best bet is to cover your vulnerable plants with newspaper overnight (weigh it down with stones at the corners to stop it blowing away) and with any luck they'll be safe. You could use horticultural fleece if you have any, or even old net curtains.

Pocket facts

There's a folklore belief that a cold snap occurs from 11 to 13 May each year, and that crops shouldn't be planted until after this. Interestingly, this belief is borne out by the facts more often than not; about six years out of 10 the middle of May sees a cold spell over much of the country.

～ Autumn frosts ～

The first widespread frosts in the central UK usually happen in September, though the closer to the coast you are the later the first frost is likely to occur (but no guarantees). The extreme western edges often escape frost until November. Interestingly the first extensive frosts are often, though not 100 percent reliably, preceded by north to north-westerly winds.

Here's a list of the most likely month of the year for a first ground frost up and down the country, though keep an eye on the weather forecast as these are not guarantees. A ground frost will damage only the most tender plants, but serves as a warning that you need to protect other plants against more damaging air frosts if you haven't done so already. The pattern of arrival of autumn is much the same as for spring in reverse, so the last places to get frosts are the south west and areas near the coast. Again, high ground will tend to see frosts earlier than lower lying land.

Plymouth	late October
Bristol	late October
Cardiff	late October
London	early October
Cambridge	early October
Birmingham	late September
Liverpool	late October
Leeds	late September
Edinburgh	late September
Isle of Skye	early November
Wick	early October

✦ Which plants are vulnerable in autumn?

The flowering plants most at risk from frost in the autumn include:

some penstemons *helichrysum petiolare*
argyranthemum *heliotrope*
chocolate cosmos *osteospermum*
fuchsia *pelargonium (geranium)*

Certain fruit, vegetables and herbs must be harvested before the first frost or they will be damaged. These are many of the same ones which you had to wait until after the last spring frosts to plant out, and include:

basil *potato* *tomatoes*
courgettes *squash*
French beans *runner beans*

Marrows and *pumpkins* are strictly speaking vulnerable to frost but they are so thick-skinned that in most areas they will be fine for a while after the first frosts. They won't last all winter though, and are usually harvested in the autumn.

Rule of thumb 🌿

It is chiefly non-native plants from warmer countries that need protection from frost.

So, the weather forecast has just told you that the first frosts of autumn are expected, and you're standing looking round at a garden dotted with tender plants. What do you do? You have two basic options for those plants which need help to survive the winter: protect them, or move them inside.

Protection

You need to put some kind of cover or protective packing over smaller plants or around the base of larger plants (such as *tree ferns*). You could use:

o fleece
o compost
o leaf mould
o hay, straw or bracken
o sawdust

Don't forget to check them through the winter and replace the protection if necessary. Cloches are good for protecting from cold winds but will only protect against the lightest frosts. If the weather gets sharper, cover the cloche with straw and keep it in place with netting or an open bamboo cloche.

Some shrubs, trees and climbers need protecting from frost or cold winds through the winter. The most common examples include:

abutilon   *orange tree*   *solanum wendlandii*
lemon tree   *palm*   *tree fern*
lemon verbena   *plumbago auriculata*

It can be a tricky task to wrap up a tree or a climber for the winter – trickier than most of your Christmas wrapping. If you grow the plants in pots you can move them (see below) but if not, you can pack the base of leafy plants with straw and then wrap them in sacking or hessian.

Moving

Clearly it helps to think ahead here, because the easiest way to move something is to have it growing in a pot. Depending on the plant you can either move it to a cold greenhouse, a warm greenhouse (if you have one) or into the house. Obviously you'll need to water it through the winter.

Pocket facts

A south facing slope warms up in sunshine much faster than level ground. In winter a slope of 15 degrees facing towards the sun is enough to double the heat received from the sun.

And what if you do get caught by an unexpected frost and have unprotected plants in the garden? Well, you may of course lose some plants but, before you give up all hope, try spraying water on the leaves of frosted plants before the sun gets to them. It will thaw them out slower which may help save them.

⮌ Greenhouses

You can move plants into a greenhouse, or grow them there, in order to keep them protected from frost. Greenhouses can be cold (unheated) or warm (heated), and some plants are more suited to one than the other. The following lists are a general guide, but if you live in a particularly cold area some plants that would normally be happy with a cold greenhouse may need to be overwintered in a warm greenhouse. Likewise some borderline plants which can survive outside in warmer parts of the country might be better off in a cold greenhouse if you live in the frozen north.

Plants you can overwinter in a cold greenhouse

This just keeps out the frost but not the cold. It's mostly suitable for plants which are listed as half-hardy. If there's a very cold forecast you might do well to provide a small amount of heat, or even just leave the light on. Or you can line the greenhouse with bubble wrap, with the bubbles against the glass. Some plants that need to overwinter in a cold greenhouse include:

chocolate cosmos	*oleander*	*rhodochiton*
cobaea	*pelargonium (geranium)*	*tender lavenders*
fuchsia	*pineapple sage*	

And a couple of borderline candidates which might need a warm greenhouse in colder parts of the country: *plumbago* and *citrus trees*. You can also use a cold greenhouse for some hardy annuals if you sowed them in the autumn, such as *sweet peas*.

Plants to overwinter in a warm greenhouse

Warm greenhouses are usually kept at around 5°C, although you can increase the temperature if you're growing something which needs more warmth. As well as any plants you grow in it all year round, a warm greenhouse will be suitable for overwintering:

abutilon	echeveria	solanum wendlandii
datura	gazania	

Planting

For most gardeners, planting is one of the most enjoyable jobs in the garden. It enables you to exercise your creative tendencies in choosing where to plant your latest acquisition, and you can see immediate results. If you have something that needs planting out at the moment, the key questions will be when, where and how.

∾ When to plant ∾

Different kinds of plants are planted out at different times of year. If it's January and you have a packet of *sunflower* seeds in your hand, go and put it away for a few months and find something else to do in the garden for now.

Here's a rough guide to the times of year you should be planting out different kinds of plants:

Perennial	Generally between October and March, though before Christmas is best to establish their roots. Pot grown plants can be planted at any time but may need extra watering if planted at other times.
Hardy annual (from seed)	Sow straight into the ground in spring.

Half hardy annual (from seed)	Sow indoors and plant out after risk of frost.
Biennial	Sow in the first year, usually in seed trays, and plant out in autumn to flower next summer.

Note: for more on sowing seeds see the section on propagation on page 36.

If you've just bought a plant you should plant it out as soon as possible. So what if you can't find time to do it straight away? Well, if it's bare rooted you should heel it in until you can plant it out (dig a hole and plant it temporarily so its roots are in the soil). Although pot grown plants can wait longer to be planted, you need to keep an eye on them and make sure they don't dry out, especially in hot dry weather. And a few more guidelines:

o Don't put plants into ground which is either frost bound, saturated or dry.

o The soil should be damp, though not wet enough to clog.

o If you're planting in dry weather you need to water the ground well the night before. If you're just about to plant out in dry weather – sorry, ideally you should wait until tomorrow to plant.

o Don't plant out in the heat of the day. For plants, heat equals stress. The best times to plant are evening or afternoon, after the sun has left the chosen spot, or on a dull day.

∾ Choosing where to plant your ∾ latest acquisition

Professional garden designers always know exactly what will go where before they start planting. But surely even they are prone to the odd impulse buy, or a cutting of something that takes their fancy? Certainly the rest of us are and, regardless of what the professionals do, we're frequently guilty of buying a plant or begging a cutting with scarcely a thought for where we'll actually put it. So if you're standing in the middle of your garden with an exciting new plant you're thrilled with but unsure quite where to put, here are a few tips to help you decide.

To begin with, some parts of your garden are sunnier or shadier than others, and your new plant will prefer full sun, partial shade or full shade, so you'll need to take this into account. Here's a quick guide to the different directions your garden – or individual flower bed – may face, and which suits what kind of plant:

North	Cold and sunless, but ideal for many shade loving plants. It's usually damper as well, which appeals to many of the same plants.
South	Hot, sunny and dry. Perfect for plants from hot dry climates, such as many herbs, but too much for some plants. Good for grey-leaved plants.
East	Early sun but often cold winds (unless in your case the east facing part of the garden is very sheltered). The sudden heat of the early sun after a frost can be too much of a contrast for some more tender plants.

West	Later, warmer sun and generally more protected from harsh winds. It's an ideal spot for those plants which can tolerate shade in the morning and enjoy the sun.

Once you've decided which way your new plant should face, here are a few other considerations:

o Bear in mind the relative heights of this plant and its neighbours – their eventual height if any of them aren't yet full grown – and position them so the taller ones don't obscure the shorter ones, or deprive them of light or air.

o The soil under trees tends to be very dry and poor as they take most of the water and nutrients, so only a few plants will be happy here.

o Think about whether you want to fill a gap where nothing else much flowers at the same time of year as this plant, or whether you want to use it to help make a certain corner of your garden a mass of colour during a particular season.

o If this plant is going to flower at the same time as its neighbours, think about whether the flowers will look good together.

o Foliage is an important factor too. Some leaves look particularly good against other plants. For example, plants with purple foliage will look good next to pink flowers.

o Plants with contrasting shapes and foliage look more interesting together than a mass of similarly shaped and coloured plants. For example, tall spiky *iris* leaves will go well next to the soft bronze or purple mound of *heuchera* foliage.

o If this plant is very fragrant, it might be sensible to plant it close to the house or a path where you'll get the best opportunity to enjoy the scent.

o If this plant is going to be at its best during the colder part of the year when you don't get out so much, plant it where you can see it from the house or will walk past it on your way to and from the front door.

↬ When will it flower?

Flowers are the mainstay of many gardens, and most plants are at their best when they are flowering. If you're laying out a bed or moving plants around, it can be useful to know when they're going to flower. That way you can put them with neighbours which will set them off, or make sure that each part of the garden has something of interest at most times of year.

So before you plant your latest purchase from the garden centre, or move that plant, here's a quick guide to the best months for a range of popular garden plants. If you've just bought a plant with a label on it, it should tell you when it will flower. However, if you're trying to decide what to put it next to, this guide will tell you roughly when its neighbours will be at their best.

Bear in mind that these times do vary across the country, and even locally depending on whether your garden is exposed or sheltered. Indeed, they may even vary slightly from one part of your garden to another. (I have an old tree in my garden which is taller than the house. The leaves at the exposed top of it appear a good 10 days later than those at the bottom, which are sheltered by the house.) A cold winter can delay early spring flowering, and a mild one can see daffodils flowering in January in warmer parts of the country. Nevertheless, this is a good general guide to when you can expect your plants to be looking their best.

January

clematis cirrhosa	garrya elliptica	wintersweet
cyclamen coum	heather	

February

aconite	daphne mezereum	snowdrop
anemone blanda	hepatica nobilis	tulipa kaufmanniana
chionodoxa	iris reticulata	winter heliotrope
cyclamen coum	oriental hellebore	witch hazel

March

aubretia	daffodil	saxifrage
common gorse	hellebore	tulipa tarda
crocus	chaenomeles	
cyclamen coum	primrose	

April

aubretia	doronicum	pasque flower
clematis alpina	honesty	rosemary
common broom	laburnum	tulip

May

aquilegia	French lavender	peony
dicentra	lilac	pot marigold
forget-me-not	lupin	tulip

June

ballota	lady's mantle	opium poppy
Canterbury bells	larkspur	rose
catmint	love-in-a-mist	sweet pea
cotton lavender	madonna lily	
laburnum	meconopsis	

July

delphinium	large-flowered clematis	regal lily
foxglove	martagon lily	salvia patens
hyssop	nasturtium	sweet pea

August

basil	evening primrose	rudbeckia
ceratostigma	fuchsia	sunflower
cosmos	gladiolus	
dahlia	Japanese anemone	

September

abelia grandiflora	chrysanthemum	toad lily
aster	clerodendrum bungei	
autumn crocus	cyclamen neopolitanum	

October

autumn cyclamen	Kaffir lily
autumn gentian	nerine
cotoneaster (berries)	rose hip (berries)

November

cornus (bright stems)	viburnum bodnantense
crab apple (fruit)	camellia Williamsii 'Donation'
pyracanthus (berries)	prunus subhirtella

December

Christmas rose	mimosa
cyclamen coum	winter iris
lonicera fragrantissima	winter jasmine
mahonia 'Charity'	

Broadly speaking, as you may have noticed from this list, certain types of plants tend to be at their best at certain times of year. Of course there are exceptions, but as a rough guide:

bulbs	*spring and autumn*
annuals	*midsummer onwards*
biennials	*early summer onwards*
perennials	*late spring onwards*

Whoops!

If you find you've planted something in the wrong place, don't despair. You can always dig it up and replant it in a better spot. Ideally you should do this when it's dormant but that isn't always possible, though don't try to move evergreens between May and September (late October is best). If you need to move it at any time of year, don't dig it up until you have the hole ready to plant it into, and then follow the guidelines below for planting out pot grown plants.

∿ How to plant ∿

The broad principles of planting are to cause the plant as little stress as possible, and to plant it in conditions which are as natural and as conducive to its health as possible. The way you apply these principles varies slightly according to whether you are planting bare rooted plants, pot grown plants or bulbs, and there are also specific additional factors if you're planting into containers, so all these are set out below.

↬ *How to plant bare rooted plants*

Apart from the odd plant you've begged from someone else and the soil around it fell off in the car on the way home, most bare rooted plants will be ones you've bought during the winter months when they're dormant. These are generally shrubs and trees. If you've ordered from a specialist nursery you may have placed the order months ago for delivery at this time of year. You may not have been expecting it to turn up this week, but now it's here you need to deal with it promptly.

o The soil should be well broken up, and you need to dig a hole about twice the size of the rootball.

o Untangle the roots and spread them out so they aren't crowded or twisted (you don't have to spend hours teasing out every last one, you're just freeing them up and giving them space). You'll also need to fork over the base of the hole so the soil is loose for the roots to get down into.

o If the plant needs staking, for example a fruit tree, put the stake in now so you can't damage the roots doing it later.

o Put the rootball into the hole and partially fill the hole – just enough to cover the roots – with soil mixed with some compost or bonemeal (see pages 53 and 96 for composts and fertilisers). Then give the plant a little shake to get rid of any air pockets; if a root hits an air pocket it will get no nutrients from it.

o Fill the hole with the soil/compost mix bit by bit, firming it down with your heel or knuckles as you go.

o Water well, especially if the weather is hot and dry.

o Come back in an hour or so when the water has soaked in and lightly firm the soil again. If you have heavy soil make sure you don't overdo this.

Rule of thumb 🌿

The best planting time for bare rooted plants is November to March (and ideally before Christmas) when they are dormant. You can plant out pot grown plants at any time.

⊸ *How to plant pot grown plants or plants grown from seed in trays*

Most of the plants you buy from the garden centre, the school fair or the local market stall will be in pots. You can plant these out at any time of year, and here's how.

o Water the plant well in the pot a couple of hours before planting.

o Dig a hole about twice the size of the pot.

o If the plant is large, such as a rose, clematis, shrub or tree, mix some compost, fertiliser or bonemeal in with the soil you've taken out of the hole (see pages 53 and 96 for composts and fertilisers). If this plant needs particularly good drainage, add some grit or sand to the mix.

o Put a splash of water in the hole.

o If the plant needs staking immediately (any plant prone to flop which is starting to get quite tall, such as *delphinium*) put the stake in now, before the plant goes in the hole, so you can't damage the roots.

o Put one hand flat across the top of the pot with the plant stem securely between your outspread fingers. You're about to turn the whole thing upside down and you don't want the plant to become separated from the soil in the pot, or the roots to be disturbed more than necessary. Now upend the pot so the plant is top down but held firmly in place by your hand.

o With the other hand, tap firmly on the bottom of the pot. This should free the pot from the soil so you can lift it clean off leaving the plant, in its soil, upside down in your hand.

o Plants may be 'pot bound' – in other words have a mass of tangled roots suggesting they should have been moved to a larger pot some time ago. If so, squeeze the rootball gently and tease out the roots before planting.

o Carefully turn the plant and soil the right way up and place it in the hole so the soil at the top of the plant is flush with the soil you're planting into. Backfill with the soil or – in the case of larger plants – the soil/compost mix. Firm the soil down as you go to make sure there are no air pockets.

o Water the plant in well, especially if the weather is hot and dry. However don't waterlog it; if the soil is already wet from rain you may not need to water much at all.

A good tip to help make sure that the plant is at the right depth is to lay a bamboo cane across the hole. The top of the soil in the pot should be level with the surrounding ground. For bare rooted plants, the roots should all be below ground, and any grafting mark on fruit trees should be above ground level.

Pocket facts

Clematis are prone to a mysterious disease known as clematis wilt, which causes them to wither and die. You can prevent this by planting your clematis about two inches deeper in the flower bed than it is in the pot you've bought it in.

Planting bulbs

o Spring flowering bulbs dry out over the summer so you'll need to plant them as soon as possible if you've just bought them.

o There's no need to water in bulbs. Just make a hole the right size for the bulb, put the bulb in with the end which is going to shoot pointing upwards, and cover over again.

o If you want the plants to look natural when they come up – for example *crocuses* or *daffodils* under a tree – throw a handful of bulbs on the planting area so they land in a random arrangement and plant them where they land.

o If you want to plant or move *snowdrops* or *aconites* these are best planted 'in the green'; that is, just after they have flowered and are still in leaf.

Rule of thumb ❧

As a rough guide, bulbs should be planted at a depth of two to three times their own height.

❧ Planting into containers

There's not a lot of difference between planting into the ground and planting into a container, but there are a few additional points you need to note in order to fool the plant into thinking it's growing in natural conditions. Drainage is the big issue with pots as you don't want them to become waterlogged in heavy rain.

o Make sure the container you are planting into has drainage holes. If it doesn't, drill a few holes in it.

o Put a layer of drainage material in the bottom of the pot (small stones, broken flower pots etc) so there is plenty of space for drainage. As a guide, for a roughly standard flower pot this should occupy about the bottom quarter to third of the pot.

o Plant in the recommended type of compost (see pages 53 and 96 for compost types).

o Water well.

∽ Planting distances ∽

So you've bought a strip of plants from the garden centre, or you've got a group of three or four plants to put together. How far apart should you space them?

o Space plants out widely enough for the final size of the plant, even if it looks as if there's a lot of bare earth at the moment.

o Shrubs and trees will obviously take a long time to grow so you can plant around them for now, but remember to put in only annuals or short lived plants.

o If you plant too close together, the smaller plants will get crowded out as the larger ones take all the light and nutrients.

Summer bedding plants can be planted reasonably close to achieve a mass effect. If you're sowing annuals from seed, thin them out when they start to come up to give the survivors more space. Here are some examples of how far apart to space annuals and biennials:

6" apart	*linaria, lobelia, nemesia, scarlet flax*
8" apart	*bellis, dwarf snapdragon, sweet William, night-scented stock, annual pink*
12" apart	*larger strains of snapdragon, calendula, Canterbury bell, cornflower, heliotrope, tobacco plant*

| 15" apart | begonia, larkspur, honesty |

| 1-2' apart | foxglove, lavatera, nicotiana sylvestris |

| 2-3' apart | sunflower |

Note: see the section on 'Plants for food' for planting distances between fruits and vegetables, page 64.

Propagating

Plants can be expensive to buy, and not always easy to find in the local garden centre. So if you want more plants the best option is often to create them yourself. You may want to increase your single lavender plant into a hedge, grow next year's sweet peas from the seeds of this year's, produce spare plants for friends, or grow a favourite new discovery from seeds or cuttings donated by someone else. Or perhaps you've bought seeds rather than young plants and want to know how to grow them. Propagating most common garden plants is actually pretty simple.

However, you may find yourself standing over the plant you've chosen to propagate and wondering what to do next. Should you divide it? Take cuttings? Collect seed? And when and how should you do it? Here's a quick rundown of the basic methods of propagating and when you would use them.

To begin with, here's a quick checklist to help you decide which of the basic methods suits what plant:

Seeds	Most plants, but it's a very slow process for larger plants such as shrubs, climbers and trees and other methods may be faster and/or more reliable. Best for annual and biennial flowering plants, and herbaceous perennials.

Dividing	Most perennials.
Layering	Some woody plants that put out shoots eg *clematis, magnolia, winter jasmine, hydrangea, akebia, wisteria*.
Cuttings	Most perennials which don't lend themselves to dividing, in other words they don't grow from a clumping base which expands as they age. You can also take cuttings from many plants which can also be divided. You can get more new plants with cuttings than by dividing, and you don't have to disturb the original plant.
Root cuttings	Some herbaceous plants such as *phlox, anchusa, romneya, oriental poppy, hellebore*.
Grafting	Mostly trees and it's hideously complicated, so you'll need a specialist book to help you I'm afraid. The best rule of thumb is don't do it unless you're sure you want to learn a complicated new skill.

∼ Seeds ∼

This is the best low cost method of generating new plants which you don't already have. Dividing, layering and taking cuttings are all very well, but you need a parent plant to begin with. You can buy packets of seeds for plants you don't already have much more cheaply than you can buy a young plant.

When?

Unsurprisingly, spring is the time to sow seeds. If you're

growing seed that you've bought in a packet, it should tell you when to sow it. However if you've collected the seed yourself, or mislaid the packet, here's a rough guide:

o Most tender plants which need to be started indoors are sown in February or March.

o Most hardy annuals are sown in about March or April, directly into the soil where you want them to flower.

o Herbaceous plants are usually started off indoors in about February or March, or outside in late spring.

How?

You've got your packet of seeds, now what are you going to do with it?

Rule of thumb 🐝

If you're starting off seedlings indoors, sow small seeds thinly into trays of some kind and larger seeds individually into pots.

o Use a clean seed tray or pot and fill it with compost (either seed compost or multi-purpose). Firm it down gently; you don't want to squish all the air out, but you want to get rid of large air pockets.

o If you're sowing directly into the ground, break the soil up very fine before scattering the seed.

o Scatter the seed thinly over the surface and cover with a thin layer (about a quarter of an inch) of compost. If the seed is very fine you may find it easier to mix it with sand and then sprinkle it – this makes it easier to spread the seed out evenly.

o Water thoroughly.

o Some seeds need a lot of warmth (a windowsill, plastic propagator or plastic bag tied round the pot). The packet should tell you. A few, such as meconopsis, even need cold to germinate and the packet will instruct you to put the seed tray in the fridge (try not to spill compost on tonight's supper).

o Some seeds such as *nemesia*, *pansies* and *verbena* for example, do best in the dark so you will need to cover the tray or pot with a sheet of board or black plastic.

o If your seeds say they need both warmth and darkness, put them in the airing cupboard (try not to spill compost on your clean sheets).

o Seeds of other plants, including *snapdragons*, *tobacco plants* and *petunias*, will tell you on the packet that they want maximum light. So put them on the windowsill. Avoid a south facing window, however, if the weather is very sunny.

Now you've got your seeds planted, you can leave them to germinate, making sure you water them so they don't dry out. Some seeds will shoot within two or three days, others may take weeks.

o As soon as the seeds have germinated (ie the shoots start to appear) remove any covering and bring the seedlings into the light, but not direct full sunshine.

o The seedlings will initially produce a pair of leaves which don't look like that plant's normal leaves. Wait until the next leaves – their 'real' leaves – have developed before you prick the plants out into individual pots to give them plenty of space.

o Never pick up a seedling by the stem as it is so easily damaged. Loosen the soil around the base and root of the seedling with a small fork or, in the case of very small seedlings, a pencil or similar. Then lift up the seedling by a leaf in order to transplant it.

o Keep watering your seedlings regularly. As they grow into strong plants, and the weather starts to warm up, harden the plants off (see below) before planting them out.

Pocket facts

It has been scientifically demonstrated that seedlings will grow stronger if you brush your hand over them a few times each day.

∿ Dividing ∿

This isn't rocket science: the gist of dividing is that you take one plant and divide it into two or more.

When?

Is now a good time? If it's winter, yes. Plants should be divided when they are dormant to minimise the ill effects of disturbance and damage.

How?

o You need to dig up the whole plant to do this.

o Then take two garden forks and drive them, back to back, down through the centre of the plant (this is much less damaging than using a spade).

o Lever the forks against each other to pull the clump apart. If you want to divide the plant into more than two, you can repeat the process with the smaller clumps you've created.

o Sometimes the old plant centre is worn out and the edges have far more new shoots. If this is the case, throw away the middle of the clump and divide the outside sections.

o Replant the sections in their new positions and water them in to wash the soil around the roots.

∾ Layering ∾

This method involves creating a new plant as a kind of satellite still attached to the parent plant. Once it is established you can separate the two and you have a new young plant.

When?

Do this at the beginning of the growing season – usually around March – especially with woody plants such as *magnolia* and *clematis*.

How?

o Choose a well grown shoot which has not flowered.

o Make a small cut on the underside of the shoot (where the roots will grow from).

o Pin the shoot to the ground with a peg of some kind, and with the cut pressing into the soil.

o Cover a couple of inches of the shoot with soil where it's pegged down, and water it.

o Once the shoot begins to show strong new growth you can sever it from the parent plant and transplant to its new position.

∽ Cuttings ∽

This method is used for perennial plants. You literally cut a shoot off and then encourage it to regenerate into a new plant. There are three different kinds of cuttings which need to be treated differently (see table below):

Softwood cuttings	These are cuttings taken from green, sappy stems of plants such as *fuchsia*, *pelargonium (geranium)*
Half ripe cuttings	This is from mostly green material but with a small amount of woody material in it, from plants such as *escallonia*, *hydrangea*
Hardwood cuttings	These are all woody such as *willow*, *poplar*, *sambucus*, *blackcurrant*

When?

But is now a good time to do it? The best time to take most cuttings is after the end of the flowering period and ideally take them from a non-flowering stem or shoot. So you can take softwood and half-ripe cuttings from spring flowering plants such as *aubretia* and *alpine phlox* in June, and from later flowering plants in late summer or early autumn. Since you want the shoot to grow it's no good taking the cutting when the plant is dormant.

However, woody cuttings should be taken when the plant is dormant, in November.

To answer the question 'when' more specifically, you should take cuttings early in the morning or at least on a dull day. Wrap them in damp newspaper and keep them in the fridge if you haven't got time to deal with them immediately.

How?

o You need to cut off a shoot about 3-5 inches long from the tip of a healthy shoot that has no flowers on it (so the cutting can put all its strength into growing roots).

o Trim it off just below a leaf joint, and remove the lowest leaves.

o For woody plants such as lavender you can pull off a suitable shoot in such a way that a small part of the stem below peels off on one side of it, creating a 'heeled' cutting.

o Fill a pot with appropriate compost (see pages 53 and 96) or multi-purpose compost mixed about 3:1 with sharp sand. Hardwood cuttings can go straight into a section of a nursery bed outside which has sharp sand dug into it.

o Push the cutting into the edge of the compost, between the compost and the pot. You can put several cuttings in the same pot.

o Put the pot inside a clear plastic bag to conserve moisture for a week to 10 days, and put it in a warm, well lit place out of direct sunlight.

o When the cutting has rooted and is showing signs of growing, you can transplant it to a larger pot and grow it on before planting it out.

Here's a quick recap of when to take the different kinds of cuttings and where to put them:

	When	*Where*
Softwood	After flowering	In a pot in a warm place
Half ripe	After flowering	In a pot in a warm place
Hardwood	November	Outside in a nursery bed

∼ Root cuttings ∼

As the name implies, root cuttings involve taking a piece of the root and encouraging it to shoot and create a new plant.

When?

In this case you want the plant to be dormant when you take the cutting, so the time to do it is between November and April for plants such as *phlox*, *anchusa*, *oriental poppy*. Some late winter flowering plants such as *hellebores* are dormant in late autumn and early winter, so this is the time to take root cuttings from these plants.

How?

o Uncover part of the root system and cut off a 2-3 inch section of root.

o Regardless of its precise position in the soil, treat the end which was nearest to the base of the plant as the 'top' and the other end as the 'bottom' of the cutting. Cut the top end off square and trim the bottom end on the diagonal so you can tell which end is which.

o Plant the root cutting vertically in a bed or pot of sandy loam (add sand if your own soil isn't suitable) with the squared end upwards. Cover it with an inch of sand.

o Water moderately until shoots appear and then a little more often.

o Once the new plant is established, plant it into its final position.

～ Using a greenhouse or cold frame ～ (or windowsill)

A greenhouse is really useful if you want to start sowing seeds early, although a warm, well lit windowsill is just as good if you don't have a greenhouse. You can boost the temperature even more by covering the seed trays or pots with glass or putting them inside plastic bags until the seeds start to shoot.

～ Hardening off ～

Your tender young seedlings will find it rather a jolt going straight out into the cold, windy garden from the comfort of a greenhouse or windowsill, so you need to harden them off gradually. A cold frame makes an excellent halfway house, opening the lid a little further each day, but if you don't have one there are other ways to accustom your growing seedlings to the real world:

o Put your seedlings outside on warm days only to begin with, and bring them in at night.

o Cover them with plastic bags (with holes punched in them) when you first put them outside.

o Put them in an unheated garden shed or a garage, with enough light for them to grow healthily.

Once your plants are used to the outside temperatures you can plant them out in the garden.

Looking after plants

U nfortunately, of course it's not enough just to plant a few plants in your garden, sit back and watch them grow. They need attention. Then again, maybe that's fortunate since tending the garden is arguably more enjoyable for many of us than simply sitting in it. At some times of year, though, you may wish the balance between the two were slightly better organised.

There's always plenty to do looking after your garden (see 'Monthly jobs' on page 150), and this section is a quick *aide-memoire* to help you with today's jobs from pruning or deadheading to staking or watering.

∼ Pruning ∼

It's always worth bearing in mind that gardeners prune for their own benefit, not for the plant's. After all, plants don't get pruned in the wild (though they may be grazed, frosted or damaged). They do, of course, get big and untidy which is what pruning aims to control. Just remember that if you never prune your plants you won't kill them; the worst case scenario is a bit of a mess, and you can almost always put it right next time.

The critical factor in how you prune a plant is to do with how it grows. For example, if a plant flowers on new wood, the aim is to encourage lots of new growth so as to have plenty of flowers eg *buddleia, clematis viticella*. Equally, if a plant naturally grows slowly and tidily, it will need little or no pruning, eg *camellia, magnolia*.

Below is a rough and ready guide to pruning the common types of garden plant which need it. There may well be obscure varieties of some of these which have their own specialist requirements, but the guidelines below will almost always hold true and, where they don't, they won't do your plant any serious harm.

✌ The basic technique of pruning

You know what to prune, you just can't remember how to do it. Well, here's what you need to know:

o Use secateurs.

o Prune each stem back to just above a healthy outward facing bud or shoot.

o Make a clean cut that is almost square, but slopes slightly away from the bud. This leaves a minimum healing surface for the shoot, and also means that any water will run off away from the bud.

✌ When to prune

Apart from any more specific information below for particular plants, here's how to know when to prune:

o *Shrubs, roses, clematis, climbers that flower in winter, spring or early summer:* These generally flower on stems which grew last year. Prune them after flowering to encourage them to put out more growth ready to flower on next year.

o *Shrubs, roses, clematis, climbers that flower in summer or autumn*. These almost always flower on new growth, so you want as much new growth as possible. Prune them in late winter, just before the growing season starts, to stimulate growth for flowers later in the year.

The only significant exception to this is evergreen hedges – see the Hedges section on page 107.

Rule of thumb ❧

Save winter pruning until late in the season (late February/early March) to reduce the risk of new shoots getting frosted.

↬ Shrubs

Why do you want to prune your shrub? Here are the main reasons for pruning and the broad game plan that each requires:

o *It's too big.* Only you know how large you want this plant. However be aware that pruning will stimulate new growth so you'll need to take it back a long way to give it room to grow without becoming oversized again too quickly.

o *It's out of shape.* In this case choose which branches and shoots to remove to regain the shape you want. You can take the hedge trimmer or shears to most shrubs without doing any long term damage, but you may not get so many flowers for the next year. If you want flowers as well, prune stem by stem with secateurs.

o *It's getting leggy at the bottom with all the leaves at the top.* The solution to this is to cut the shrub down to about 6" from the ground, causing it to reshoot lower down. This works well with deciduous shrubs, though some evergreens won't respond well, especially acid lovers such as *rhododendron*.

o *There are dead stems or branches.* You need to prune out the dead wood, taking each stem back to a healthy shoot or bud. Removing dead wood helps prevent disease.

o *The branches are getting dense and tangled.* Prune this shrub so that the centre of it is fairly open, and no branches are crossing and rubbing against each other (which can produce wounds which may attract disease).

o *Variegated shrubs are producing all-green shoots.* Remove the offending shoots.

✤ Roses

There are five broad categories of roses, each with its own pruning style. Make sure you know what kind of rose you have if you're unsure. Actually, having said previously that it's not a good idea to prune with a hedge trimmer, in the case of roses tests have shown that it works very well and gives a good show of flowers the following year, though the stems can look tangled and messy in winter. You will still need to prune more carefully every couple of years to remove dead or criss-crossing branches.

Hybrid tea *produces a single flower on each stem*	Prune fairly heavily in March
Floribunda *produces many flowers on a single stem*	Prune lightly in March
Shrub rose *large loose growing bushes*	Prune only to remove weak, diseased or damaged wood

Climbing rose *produces strong stems from any part of the plant and can grow very large*	Prune in spring by cutting back the side flower shoots to two or three buds from the stem
Rambling rose *produces strong stems from the base and rarely grows above about 3 metres/10 '*	Cut back flowering stems to the ground immediately after flowering and tie in new shoots to replace them. If you're growing a rambler for its ornamental hips in the autumn wait until early spring to prune it

Remember to remove all the prunings. You can bet that if you leave just one thorny stem on the ground, it will get you next time you're weeding.

⌁ Clematis

These fall into three basic categories for pruning.

Early flowering species *eg alpina, macropetala*	Don't prune
Early large flowered hybrids *eg Henryi, Madame le Coultre*	Very light prune in early spring
Late flowering – hybrids and species *eg Jackmanii, texensis*	Cut hard back to within 10" (25cm) of the ground in late February/early March

⌁ Climbers

Broadly speaking, you can do as you please with climbers

you don't grow for their flowers, such as ivy or *Virginia creeper*. Just clear them back to the size you want at any time of year. When it comes to flowering climbers such as *passion flower*, *jasmine*, *akebia* or *solanum* you need to follow the guidelines on page 47 about pruning according to when they flower.

✑ *Fruit trees*

In theory you need never prune your fruit trees. However, if you keep them in good shape, especially removing dead and diseased branches and any that rub against each other, they will fruit better than if you leave them to do their own thing. Pruning for the first three years – if you choose to do it – is quite complicated if you're not an expert, and you'd be best off looking it up in a gardening encyclopedia or specialist fruit tree book.

Apples and *pears* should be pruned as other plants (see page 47), unless you're growing cordon, espalier or fan trained trees in which case I'm afraid you're beyond the scope of this book and on your own when it comes to the technique. As far as timing goes, however, here's a guide:

Free standing	Prune November to March, when dormant
Cordon	Prune late July
Espalier/fan trained	Prune leaders in November and laterals between July and September

If you have a *plum* tree it shouldn't need pruning unless there is dead wood or criss-crossing branches. If so, prune it on a dry, still day between June and August, and never in winter or you risk something called silver leaf disease which you don't want. The same applies to other varieties of stone fruit such as *damsons* and *cherries*.

～ Deadheading ～

This simply means removing the dead flowerheads from plants, as you probably know. But why would you do it? And do you have to remove every flowerhead in the garden? There are three main reasons to deadhead:

o *To improve the look of the garden.* By mid-autumn, however, it's a friendly idea to leave plenty of seedheads as they provide winter food for birds and other wildlife.

o *To encourage more flowers.* If you deadhead to prevent seeds forming and ripening, the plant will retaliate by producing more flowers. So if this particular plant isn't going to flower again anyway, there's not much point deadheading for this purpose. It's a useful thing to do for plants such as pansies and repeat flowering roses.

o *To prevent the flower from seeding.* Some flowers self-seed copiously. You may like this, but if you don't want a garden full of *opium poppies* or *ox-eye daisies* it's a wise move to remove the dead flowerheads before the seed sets.

～ Feeding ～

It's always better to feed the soil around a plant rather than applying the feed directly to the base of the plant. Feeding the soil means the food is always available to the roots when it's needed; feeding the plant generates soft growth which is attractive to pests and diseases. (See also compost section, page 96.)

✎ When should you feed?

If you regularly fertilise your soil with plenty of well rotted manure, spent mushroom compost and so on, you shouldn't need to do much extra feeding except for very greedy plants, or those with specific requirements such as acid or lime. So here's a quick reminder of when and how to use these general fertilisers:

o *Manures* Fork in in the autumn or use as a mulch in spring.

o *Compost* Your own garden compost makes a good top dressing around plants in the spring. You can also mix it into the soil when you plant roses, shrubs or deep rooted perennials.

o *Farmyard manure* Once it is well rotted you can dig this into the soil any time during the dormant season from late autumn to early spring.

o *Seaweed* Apply this to the soil in the autumn. It decomposes rapidly and is extremely nutritious.

o *Compound fertilisers* These are a mixture of potash, nitrogen and phospates. They are usually artificial but you can find natural and even organic brands. You can fork these in in the spring, and also use them to add to the soil when you're planting.

o *Bonemeal* This can be added to the soil when planting (though not for acid loving plants such as heather). It's particularly good for slow growing plants because of its slow release.

You can give additional specialist feeds to greedy plants such as *tomatoes*, and to plants which need a more acid or alkaline soil than yours is naturally. For these, you should find instructions on the packaging.

∽ Watering ∽

It's very rare that you need to water plants between October and April. They get what they need from rainfall, and from water which is retained in the soil. In hot weather, however, you may need to water many plants, especially young ones and plants which you're hoping will produce good crops for you. It's hard to see, after all, how a strawberry plant could produce juicy fruit if the soil is dry.

Rule of thumb 🌿

Don't water a plant that is wilting in the sun. Put it in the shade and cool it down before you water it. If you can't move it, wait until the spot it's in becomes cooler or shadier.

↭ Getting the most benefit for the least water

Whether your water supply is metered, you're under threat of a hosepipe ban, you're eco-minded, or you just want to save time, efficient watering is what you need. Here are a few guidelines to make sure you use as little water as possible in hot weather without your plants suffering.

o Check the forecast first. If it's going to rain it's a waste of time watering as the excess water will drain to below root depths where your plants won't benefit.

o Water below the foliage so that all the water goes into the soil where it's needed. I'm afraid this means that sprinklers are less use than a hose except for lawns or young plants.

o Use a hose with a trigger to spray the water around the base of the plant. Strong jets or heavy flows damage the soil, and a hose left trickling near the plant will encourage the water to seep straight down rather than spread out around the plant, and may expose the roots.

o Water generously once every week or two (more for some plants – see below) rather than little and often. You need the water to penetrate right down to the lower roots.

o Water in the evening so the plants and the soil get a chance to absorb it before the sun dries it out tomorrow.

o Sink a flowerpot, or plastic bottle with no bottom and no lid, almost to the rim next to thirsty plants such as tomatoes. Then fill the pot or bottle with water which will seep out of the bottom close to the roots of the plant.

o Stand pot plants under hanging baskets so they can catch the drips.

o During a hosepipe ban you can reuse water from your bath or sink to water plants as they don't mind a bit of soap or detergent. But don't use water containing bleach or salt from your washing machine or dishwasher.

⤳ How much water?

There are some categories of plants which need more or less water than others. Most well established plants, for example, shouldn't need watering even in a drought. Here's a rough guide to how often to water your plants:

Frequently (daily in very hot weather):
>   Anything newly planted
>   Leafy salad crops
>   Peas and beans when in flower

        Pots and hanging baskets
        Lawns (if you're cultivating a perfect lawn)

Occasionally (every week or two in very hot weather):
        Most soft fruit and vegetables
        Bedding plants
        Perennials which like a moist situation
        Many plants in sandy soils or very heavy clay

Never:
        Succulent plants
        Established perennials
        Ordinary lawns
        Established fruit trees
        Currants
        Ornamental grasses
        Herbs

Pocket facts

The shape of a plant's leaves gives you a good idea of where it needs the water – in other words where its roots are. Plants with central bulbs or corms, which need water around the base of the stem, tend to have tall leaves which channel the water to this point, eg *daffodil, hyacinth, gladiolus*. Plants with spreading root systems tend to have leaves which allow water to run off in a wide splay around the plant, eg *heuchera, lady's mantle*.

∾ Mulching ∾

This means adding a layer of material to the soil surface around plants to conserve moisture and suppress weeds. If you use an organic mulch such as decayed manure, leaf mould, or compost it will also add nutrients to the soil. However, you can use non-organic mulches such as black plastic sheeting or porous fibre sheeting. These are excellent for keeping the weeds down over a large area such as a vegetable plot you're preparing or underneath a path of a material such as gravel which you don't want the weeds to grow through. You can also cut holes in this kind of sheeting to plant crops such as *strawberries* through.

✧ Using organic mulches

o You can use grass cuttings as a mulch but you need to dry them out first (by spreading them out in warm weather) or they will rot.

o Shredded newspaper makes a good mulch.

o Mulch round root vegetables such as *parsnip* in the winter to keep the soil workable.

o Slugs love mulches such as bark, coco shells and leaf mould so don't mulch right up to young shoots and plants that will tempt slugs; leave a few inches around the shoots.

✧ Using non-organic mulches

o If you need moisture underneath the mulch, remember that it can't get through materials such as black plastic. So lay the sheeting after a good rainfall when it will keep the moisture in.

o Black plastic absorbs heat, and creates a wonderful home underneath for mice, voles and slugs. So it can be a problem if you put it around plants, and is more use as a long term mulch to kill off perennial weeds in a new bed. For example, six months or a year under black plastic should kill off weeds such as ground elder and bindweed, leaving the bed ready to dig over and prepare for planting.

～ Weeding ～

It's impossible to define a weed, but essentially it is any plant which is growing where you don't want it. Your weeds may be someone else's prize plant, and vice versa. However, you should know perfectly well what constitutes a weed in your own garden.

Weeding isn't many people's favourite job, but it has to be done. Quite apart from the fact that you don't want to look at them, weeds compete with your plants for food and water and may smother them. They should be removed as soon as possible and certainly before they seed, creating problems for years ahead.

Rule of thumb ✣

One year's seed is seven years' weed.

Although it is possible to kill weeds by spraying, prevention is far better than cure so aim to get the weeds out before they spread. If you have to use a spray, use a glyphosate based one which won't harm wildlife, and make sure it doesn't come into contact with any plants you don't want to lose.

Not all weeds operate in the same way, so here are a few tips for dealing with different types of weed before you get stuck in to that overgrown flower bed:

o *Annual* For example *chickweed, groundsel, scarlet pimpernel*. All you have to do with these relatively easy weeds is pull them up before they flower. If you hoe or weed after the flower is out, don't leave the weed on the flower bed as it can still seed into it.

o *Perennial* For example *dandelion, plantain, buttercup.* These weeds are deeper rooted and you need to get the whole root up in order to stop them shooting again. You'll need to dig them up as if you hoe or even pull you may leave part of the root behind.

o *Weeds which spread by rooting* In other words they send out long networks of roots which can shoot above ground at any point. For example *ground elder, bindweed, couch grass.* Oh how I hate these. If any of the root is left in the ground it will regenerate, sometimes into several plants. These weeds must be laboriously dug out or, if you're overwhelmed by them, treated with a glyphosate based weedkiller.

∾ Staking and supporting ∾

Large plants, such as newly planted trees, need a strong stake to keep them upright even in a gale. You need to attach the stake to the tree with some kind of strong tie which forms a figure-of-eight around the tree and the stake so they don't actually touch each other, or the stake will damage the tree. A couple more points if you're about to plant a tree:

o Put the stake in the hole before you plant the tree in it, so you can't damage the roots putting it in later.

o Site the stake on the side of the tree which the prevailing winds come from, so they will blow the tree away from the stake, and not on to it.

Some plants are susceptible to strong winds, or the pull of the sun and daylight, and need to be kept upright or they will flop over and collapse. Plants particularly prone to do this include *chrysanthemum, dahlia, delphinium, Michaelmas daisy, oriental poppy, peony*.

You can buy ready made plant supports, hoops and all manner of products to support herbaceous plants. But if you're in the middle of a gardening session you don't necessarily want to stop, get in the car and drive down to the local garden centre to spend decent money on something you could make for nothing. Much better is to know how to make it for nothing. Here are a couple of suggestions for on-the-spot DIY supports:

o Brushwood and small branches with plenty of fanned out twigs on them work well. Drive them into the ground so that the twigs fan round the plant.

o Put four or five sturdy sticks or bamboo canes around the plant and then tie string around and across them, to form a web which the plant can grow through.

o For some tall plants, such as *gladioli*, a single cane will do which you can then tie the flowering stem into.

⟶ When do you put the supports in?

The idea is that you should put in the support before the plant needs it, so that it will grow up through it. This means sometime in spring, depending on the plant. If you do this, the supports will be all but invisible once the plant reaches its best. Also, you can create a far more intricate and supportive network of string or other supports without the plant there to get in your way and risk damage to.

The downside of this is that the supports will look very unattractive until the plant grows. You can resolve this by using a support that is attractive in itself, such as peasticks. Or you can push the stakes deep into the ground and raise them gradually as the plant grows.

If you didn't get ahead with your staking, better late than never. If you didn't put in supports in the spring and your plant is now starting to flop, you can still support it to prevent total collapse. You'll need to be more careful that you don't damage the plant in the process.

Rule of thumb 🌿

Herbaceous plants should be supported up to about half their eventual height, or two thirds if the flower itself is heavy such as oriental poppy *or* peony.

✪ Supporting climbers

Some climbers are naturally clinging, while others have a lazier style. But even climbers with tendrils or leaves that twine round host plants or supports (such as *clematis*) need some guidance or they'll grow towards the sun and end up uneven and lopsided. So if you have a climber that is in danger of flopping rather than climbing, here are a couple of tips for supporting it:

o If you need to put up wires on a wall or fence to support your climber, these should be about 12" /30cm apart in both vertical and horizontal rows, starting about 2'/60cm from the ground. Use strong wire which will last – replacing wire after the plant has grown is a nightmare.

o Don't try to twine the climber straight into wire or trellis.

Tie the plant into it (not too tightly) and then let it find its own way.

～ Protection ～

There are probably at least a few tender plants in your garden which need protection from frosts either by bringing them indoors over the winter or by some other method. For general advice on frost protection see the 'Frosty facts' section on page 12. For advice about using a cold greenhouse, cloches or cold frames see 'Growing under glass' on page 86.

～ Picking flowers ～

One of the most delicious garden tasks is picking flowers for the house. But hold on a second, before you start snipping away, here are a few tips for cutting flowers to make sure the blooms last as well as possible, and the garden still looks good too:

o Don't pick too many from one plant – your flowers will last longer in the garden than in the house.

o Always use secateurs or gardening scissors and make a clean cut.

o Try to avoid picking flowers when the sun is on them.

o Some flowers just don't last in water, such as *hellebore, poppy, flax, japanese anemone, crocus, hollyhock*.

o If the side shoots are big enough, pick one or two. If not, pick the main flower but above where the side shoots branch out. That will encourage the side shoots to lengthen and flower.

o Cut all the stems to roughly the same length.

o Keep the finished vase in mind as you pick, so as not to find you've picked a flower you can't use. This will also help to make sure you've got all the colours you need if you're going for a colour theme rather than a glorious mixed bunch.

o Remove all the leaves that will be below the waterline in the vase.

o Flowers in a vase almost always look better with some greenery, so if you're picking flowers with no leaves on the stem (such as daffodils) pick the leaves separately, or pick greenery from other plants or shrubs.

Plants for food

Growing your own food is such a delight that it's worth doing in the smallest garden, even if it's only the odd pot of herbs. Many fruits and vegetables are pretty easy to grow, and if you have a particular passion for fresh strawberries, for example, or home made vegetable soups, you may well be growing at least a few favourites.

Not all vegetable gardening is as back-breaking as planting potatoes, but there's no denying that a fruit or vegetable garden is higher maintenance than, say, a shrubbery. And the more there is to do, the more there is to forget. So the following *aides-memoire* should help you in the kitchen garden.

Rule of thumb ❧

Try to avoid planting crops which will be ready to harvest when you're away on holiday. Choose early or late varieties if necessary.

∾ Vegetables ∾

The two things you're most likely to want a reminder of are planting distances for vegetables, and when to sow and harvest them. The following charts should give you the answers. I have no excuse for my inconsistent use of metric and imperial measurements.

↬ Planting distances

	Depth	Distance between plants	Distance between rows
Broad bean	2"	6" (15cm)	24" (60cm)
French bean	2"	4" (10cm)	18" (45cm)
Runner bean	2"	6" (15cm)	4' (120cm)
Beetroot	1"	8-10" (20-25cm)	12" (30cm)
Broccoli	1/2"	24" (60cm)	24" (60cm)
Purple sprouting broccoli	1/2"	24" (60cm)	24" (60cm)
Brussels sprout	1/2"	30" (76cm)	30" (76cm)
Spring cabbage	1/2"	18" (45cm)	18" (45cm)
Summer cabbage	1/2"	18" (45cm)	18" (45cm)
Carrot	1/2"	4" (10cm)	12" (30cm)
Cauliflower	1/2"	24" (60cm)	24" (60cm)
Celery	1/2"	8" (20cm)	36" (90cm)
Courgette	1"	3' (90cm)	3' (90cm)
Leek	1/2"	9" (23cm)	12" (30cm)
Lettuce	1/2"	9" (23cm)	12" (30cm)
Marrow	1"	3' (90cm)	3' (90cm)
Onion from seed	1/2"	4" (10cm)	12" (30cm)
Onion sets	Tops just showing	4" (10cm)	12" (30cm)

	Depth	*Distance between plants*	*Distance between rows*
Spring onion	$1/4$"	1" (15cm)	4" (15cm)
Parsnip	$1/2$"	9" (23cm)	12" (30cm)
Pea	2"	2" (5cm)	3' (90cm)
Potato	5"	15" (38cm)	24" (60cm)
Pumpkin	1"	3' (90cm)	3' (90cm)
Radish	$1/2$"	2" (5cm)	9" (23cm)
Rhubarb	6"	3' (90cm)	3-4' (90-120cm)
Shallot	1"	9" (23cm)	9" (23cm)
Spinach	$1/2$"	6" (15cm)	12" (30cm)
Swede	$1/4$"	12" (30cm)	18" (45cm)
Sweetcorn	1"	15" (38cm)	15" (38cm)
Tomato	$1/4$"	24" (60cm)	24" (60cm)
Turnip	$1/2$"	10" (25cm)	12" (30cm)

Sowing and harvesting

	Sow	Plant out (if relevant)	Harvest
Broad bean	Late autumn/early spring		Late spring/summer
French bean	Late spring/early summer		Summer
Runner bean	Late spring/early summer		Late summer
Beetroot	Mid-spring/early summer		Summer/autumn
Broccoli	Spring	Late spring/early summer	Late winter/spring
Purple sprouting broccoli	Spring	Late spring/early summer	Late winter/spring
Brussels sprout	Spring	Late spring/early summer	Autumn/winter
Spring cabbage	Late summer	Early autumn	Spring
Summer cabbage	Spring		Summer
Carrot	Spring/early summer		Summer onwards

	Sow	Plant out (if relevant)	Harvest
Cauliflower	Spring		Autumn
Celery	Spring		Autumn
Courgette	Spring	Late spring	Late summer
Leek	Spring	Early summer	Autumn onwards
Lettuce	Spring onwards		Early summer onwards
Marrow	Spring	Late spring	Summer/autumn
Onion from seed	Spring		Summer
Onion sets	Spring		Late summer
Spring onion	Early spring onwards		Late spring
Parsnip	Early spring		Autumn/winter
Pea	Early spring		Summer
Potato	Early spring		Summer onwards

	Sow	Plant out (if relevant)	Harvest
Pumpkin	Spring	Late spring	Late autumn
Radish	Early spring onwards		Spring onwards
Rhubarb	Spring (outdoors)	Autumn (move to final position)	Spring/early summer
Shallot	Early spring		Summer onwards
Spinach	Early spring onwards		Late spring onwards
Swede	Late spring/early summer		Autumn
Sweetcorn	Early spring	Late spring	Late summer
Tomato	Spring	Late spring	Late summer/autumn
Turnip	Early spring onwards		Summer

You may be wondering when early spring is, or which month is late summer? Here's a general guide, though of course if you live in the far north or deep south you may want to make allowances.

Table of seasons

Early spring	March
Spring	April
Late spring	May
Early summer	June
Summer	July
Late summer	August
Early autumn	September
Autumn	October
Late autumn	November
Early winter	December
Winter	January
Late winter	February

✧ Guidelines for specific vegetables

Most vegetables are pretty straightforward to look after. You sow them, water them, watch them grow and then harvest them. Some, however, require something slightly different, so what follows are reminders of the extra tasks for some of the most popular vegetables (including rhubarb, which honestly is a vegetable).

Celery

This needs to be earthed up in order to keep the stems white. The idea is to plant it in a trench about 12-18" (30-45cm) deep so you earth up by simply filling in the trench. It's usually done in three stages:

o In August, when the plants are at least 12" (30cm) tall, loosely tie black polythene or newspaper around the stalks to keep the earth out. Earth up about 3" (7-8cm).

o About three weeks later earth up another 6" (15cm).

o Finally, three weeks later, earth up to cover the stalks completely (but not the leaves).

Harvest from November onwards.

Leeks

Leek seedlings should be transplanted to their final growing positions in late May or June when they are about pencil thickness, and around 6-8" high (15-20cm). Make holes 6" deep (15cm) and 2" wide (5cm) with a dibber, or something the same size. Space them 6" apart (15cm) in rows which are 12" apart (30cm). Drop one seedling into each hole and fill the hole with water. Do not replace the soil.

Onions

When *onion* bulbs are reaching maturity, their leaves begin to yellow and topple over. This may be delayed in wet seasons so the tops should be bent over by hand to help the bulbs ripen. Harvest when the leaves have shrivelled.

Potatoes

Potatoes are normally grown in rows on ridges which are

formed gradually through the season by earthing up every two to three weeks. Early in the year you earth up to protect the shoots from frost. Later on the extra soil will stop potatoes growing close to the surface; if they do so the exposure to light turns them green.

Rhubarb

Although you can grow *rhubarb* from seed, it's a lengthy and unreliable process especially if you're a relative novice. It's better to propagate by root division or buy young plants.

You can force *rhubarb* to provide an early crop of tender stalks. In winter, mid-January or February, cover the plants to be forced with a dustbin, barrel, bucket or rhubarb forcer to exclude all light. Insulate this cover by packing straw or similar material inside it covering the *rhubarb* crown, or over and around the outside, to build up warmth inside. You should have stalks ready to eat in five to six weeks. Don't pick from a forced plant for the next two years.

Runner beans

Pinch out the tops when they reach the top of their support system to prevent them growing any further upwards. Incidentally, *runner bean* (and *broad bean*) roots contain nitrogen fixing bacteria which improves soil fertility for subsequent crops. So after harvesting, remove the plant tops but leave the roots in the ground and dig them in, or put them on the compost heap.

Tomatoes

You can grow bush tomatoes which require very little intervention. However if you grow cordon varieties you'll need to help them along:

o After planting them out in early June, tie each plant to its own stake.

o Remove any side shoots that develop (between the stem and a leaf).

o Once four trusses of flowers have set, pinch off the top of the plant two leaves above the fourth truss.

If you leave more flower trusses the plant will spread its energy too thinly and fewer tomatoes will have a chance to ripen before the autumn frosts.

Trailing marrows and squashes

Pinch out the growing points on the plants' lateral (side) branches when they are 24" (60cm) long. (This doesn't apply to bush varieties.)

✎ *Companion planting*

This is a method of planting which entails growing compatible plants next to each other. Some plants help keep pests in check, and a mix of plants with different tolerances to disease makes disease less likely. Some plants are also said to improve the flavour of others when grown nearby. Some instances of companion planting have more scientific evidence to back them up than others; then again, it can't hurt to plant supposedly compatible plants together and in some cases it will help.

Crop	Plant close to...
Beans	Beetroot, cabbage, carrot, sweetcorn, tomato and not onion
Beetroot	Cabbage
Broccoli	Bean, celery, onion, potato
Brussels sprout	Bean, celery, potato
Cabbage	Bean, beetroot, celery, onion, potato
Carrot	Bean, leek, onion, pea, radish, tomato
Cauliflower	Bean, beetroot, celery, onion, potato
Celery	Bean, cabbage, leek
Leek	Carrot, celery
Lettuce	Beetroot, cabbage, pea
Marrow/courgette	Bean, sweetcorn
Onion	Cabbage, carrot, lettuce, potato, tomato
Pea	Carrot, lettuce, spinach, sweetcorn, turnip
Potato	Bean, cabbage, lettuce, onion
Radish	Bean, cabbage, lettuce, pea, tomato
Spinach	Cabbage, celery, onion, pea
Tomato	Cabbage, carrot, onion, pea
Turnip	Pea

See also Herbs as companion plants on page 82.

Rule of thumb ❦

Almost any mixed planting will be more resistant to pests and diseases than block planting, which encourages pests to feast and diseases to spread.

↬ Crop rotation

The principle behind crop rotation is that different plants take different nutrients out of the soil, and put different ones back. So if you keep growing the same plants in the same place, the soil will become more and more denuded. If, on the other hand, you rotate your crops around the vegetable garden, you can make sure that each type of vegetable is followed by a different group which is compatible with the soil that has been left by the previous crops. For example, peas and beans are able to fix the nitrogen from the air in the soil, so they leave it rich in nitrates for the brassicas which follow. Crop rotation also helps to minimise pests and diseases.

This system also means that you can reduce the amount of additional feeding your crops need, since they will be planted in soil which is already rich in many of the required nutrients.

The standard crop rotation system divides the vegetable garden into three equal parts (for the four year system see below). Broadly speaking there is one section each for:

o peas and beans

o brassicas

o root vegetables

These groups are planted in succession in each of the sections, so that every three years you get back to the beginning. To be more specific, here is a longer list of which bed to plant each type of vegetable in, and what kind of feed you should give it.

Three year crop rotation

	Bed A	Bed B	Bed C
Vegetables	beans, celery, leek, lettuce, onion, peas, radish, shallot	broccoli, cabbage, cauliflower, spinach, sprouts	beetroot, carrot, parsnip, potato, swede, turnip
Feed	Manure or compost	General fertiliser (and lime if your soil is acid)	General fertiliser

The four year crop rotation system is ideal if you have room to divide your vegetable plot into four. The basic groups are:

o alliums (onion family)

o brassicas

o peas and beans

o root vegetables

Again, move each group on to the next bed in sequence, returning to the starting point after four years. As you can see, the difference between this and the three year system is that the alliums and the peas and beans have been separated.

Four year crop rotation

	Bed A	Bed B	Bed C	Bed D
Vegetables	Onion, spring onion, shallot, garlic, leek	Cabbage, Brussels sprout, cauliflower, kale, broccoli	Beans, peas	Beetroot, carrot, parsnip, potato, swede, turnip
Feed	Manure or compost	Manure or compost	General fertiliser (and lime if your soil is acid)	General fertiliser

∾ Fruit ∾

Fruit is divided into two broad categories: soft fruit and tree fruit. Tree fruit calls for little ongoing maintenance apart from occasional pruning (see page 51), however you might want more guidance than that when it comes to soft fruit. If you're standing over your blackcurrant bush with the uneasy feeling you ought to be doing something about it at this time of year but you're not sure what, or if you want to know how to encourage your rasperries to fruit, here's a quick guide to the most common soft fruits (they're in alphabetical order).

⋄ Blackberry, loganberry and other hybrid berries

Young canes appear in summer. Tie them in to the supporting wall, fence or wires, removing any weak tips. *Blackberries* and *loganberries* fruit on the previous year's growth, so you need to cut out last year's growth that has borne fruit right down to the base of the plant.

o Apply fertiliser or compost in late February.

o Harvest *blackberries* July to October (depending on the variety) and *loganberries* and other hybrid berries July to August.

o You can expect around 20lb of fruit a year from an average mature plant.

Pocket facts

Both *loganberries* and *tayberries* were bred a little over 200 years ago by crossing *blackberries* with *raspberries*. The idea is that you get the sweetness of the *raspberry* and the size and juiciness of the *blackberry*.

↔ *Blackcurrant*

Strong new shoots appear from the base of the plant. Thin out weak shoots and broken branches throughout the growing season. In winter remove about one third of the bush by cutting out badly placed and damaged wood. As *blackcurrants* fruit on last year's growth, you need to cut the fruiting branches back to a strong shoot.

o Feed with compound fertiliser in February or March.

o Harvest July to August.

o You can expect around 10lb of fruit a year from an average mature plant.

↭ Gooseberry, redcurrant and whitecurrant

The aim is to build up flowering 'spurs' on old wood. The thing about *gooseberries* is that they are naturally floppy, and the aim of the pruning is to get them to grow more upright. The other purpose is to get them into a shape which allows you to pick the fruit without lacerating your arms.

You can grow *gooseberries* in various forms such as cordons, but here are the guidelines for pruning the basic bush shape, which you should do between November and March. The pruning is slightly different for the first three years from subsequent years:

1 *First year* Cut back each branch by half to an inward and upward pointing bud. Pull out suckers round the base.

2 *Second year* Again cut back each branch by half to an inward and upward pointing bud. Select well placed shoots to form other permanent branches and cut back by a half. Pull out suckers, and remove low stems (to make it easier to reach the fruit).

3 *Third year* Shorten each branch by half to a bud facing in the required direction. Predictably, given the pruning regime, you will now have some shoots crowding the centre, so cut these out. Shorten shoots you don't need for the framework to 2" (5cm).

From the fourth year onwards, prune to keep the centre of the plant open to reduce the risk of mildew, and remove dead or diseased wood. Cut the current year's growth back to two or three buds, leaving shoots which point upwards and inwards in order to keep the plant erect.

o Feed with compound fertiliser in February.

o Harvest *gooseberries* late May to end of July (depending on the variety). Harvest *red* and *white currants* July to August.

o You can expect around 2lb of fruit a year from an average mature plant.

Loganberry see blackberry

⊕ *Raspberry*

Raspberries are usually supported on a post and wire fence. Tie them in for security against the winter wind. In the first spring you need to cut down the canes to about 9-12"/22-30cm above the ground. In subsequent years cut down last year's fruiting canes to ground level in February, and tie in the new canes about 4" apart.

Autumn fruiting raspberries bear fruit on this season's growth, so cut down all canes to ground level in February.

o Feed with potash in early spring and a mulch of compost, but leave a 4" (10cm) circle clear round the base of each cane.

o Harvest summer fruiting *raspberries* June to July, and autumn fruiting *raspberries* August to October.

o You can expect around 1.5lb of fruit a year per 12" /30cm of row from an average mature plant.

Redcurrant see gooseberry

⊕ *Strawberry*

Strawberries need no pruning, but you can cut off well rooted runners and propagate fresh plants by potting them on or planting them out. *Strawberries* are prone to pests and diseases so you shouldn't grow them on the same site for more than three or four years. You can protect *strawberries* from birds with open topped cloches with netting over the top, or in cages. Straw around the plants keeps weeds down and keeps the fruits clean, but it also provides a wonderful home for slugs and snails.

Remontant strawberries produce fruit in irregular flushes throughout the year until the frost stops them. You can prolong the crop by covering them with a cloche in autumn. They're never as good after the first year so it's best to grow on runners for next year and discard this year's plants.

o Feed sulphate of potash at the end of January. Scatter it between the plants but don't allow it to touch the plant.

o Harvest late May to October according to the type and variety.

o You can expect around 10oz of fruit a year from an average mature plant.

Alpine strawberries usually last no more than two years. Some varieties produce runners so you can propagate a fresh batch, but not all do. You can collect seed instead to grow new plants. They crop continuously, or in flushes, from June to November.

Whitecurrant see gooseberry

∾ Herbs ∾

Herbs are some of the best garden plants being both useful and attractive. Many of them smell wonderful, are edible, make good hedging plants, have medicinal properties and keep predators away from other plants.

✧ Herbs for the house

If you want to harvest herbs for drying, either for their scent or to use in the kitchen, the time to do it is:

o Just before the plant comes into flower if you want to use the leaves.

o On a sunny morning after the dew has dried.

Herbs are best used fresh for cooking, as drying reduces their flavour. However, summer herbs need to be preserved if you want to use them for winter cooking. To preserve herbs for the kitchen either:

o Hang bunches of herbs to dry in a warm place such as above the cooker or in the airing cupboard. When dry, crumble them and store in labelled, airtight jars, or

o Finely chop the herb, pack it into an ice cube tray and top up with water. Freeze and then bag up to drop into soups and stews through the winter. This preserves the flavour far better than drying (but is no good for sprinkling).

✧ Herbs as companion plants

Some herbs have a good effect in the garden, and are reckoned to improve the growth or taste of other crops, and keep predators away. Certain herbs are beneficial to certain plants. If you're wondering where to plant your *rosemary* cuttings, or how to keep blackfly off your *runner beans*, here's a guide to which plants some of the most common herbs are thought to make good companions for.

Herb	Good companion to...
Basil	Beans, cabbage, tomato
Borage	Strawberry, tomato
Caraway	Peas
Camomile	Cucumber, mint, onion
Chervil	Carrot, radish
Chive	Carrot, parsley, tomato
Coriander	Potato
Dill	Cabbage, lettuce, onion
Garlic	Carrot, tomato
Lemon balm	Tomato
Mint	Cabbage
Oregano	Cabbage, cucumber
Parsley	Carrot, chive, tomato
Rosemary	Beans, cabbage, carrot
Sage	Cabbage, carrot, strawberry, tomato
Thyme	Cabbage

∼ Moonphase planting ∼

Some people are great believers in planting according to the phases of the moon. This isn't entirely as cranky a medieval superstition as it sounds, though officially the jury is still out on whether it works.

The reasoning is that the moon's phases affect the pull of gravity, and that during the full moon the nights are lighter which significantly helps photosynthesis and other growth factors. The theory also suggests that when the moon waxes, at which time the sun and moon are moving apart (relative to the earth), it is a good time for foliage, fruit, seeds and all development above ground. The period of the waning moon (as the sun and moon move towards each other) is the best time for root development.

So what should you plant when according to this system? Well, you need to plant or sow anything that is grown for its foliage, fruit or seeds when the moon is waxing, and those plants you grow for their roots during a waning moon:

o From two days before new moon to three days before full moon (waxing period) is the time to plant all above ground plants: *salad plants, beans, peas, cabbages* etc.

o From two days before full moon to three days before new moon (waning period) is the time to plant or sow root vegetables: *potato, carrot, beetroot, onion* etc.

∾ Edible flowers ∾

If all this talk of home grown fruit and vegetables is making you peckish, you'll be pleased to know that for much of the year you can snack as you work in the garden. I'm not just talking about fruits and raw vegetables, tasty though those undoubtedly are. Many garden flowers are edible too. If you want to use them in the kitchen, pick them early in the day when the dew has just dried. You can eat small flowers whole, but with any daisy like flower you should pull the petals off gently. Then you can sprinkle them over salads.

Here are a few common garden flowers you can eat:

anchusa	*nasturtium*
borage	*pot marigold*
carnation	*primrose (but not primula)*
chicory	*rose*
cowslip	*sunflower*
daisy (bellis perennis)	*sweet bergamot*

elder   *violet*
lavender

Of course, some garden flowers are poisonous so make sure you're certain what flower you're picking. If you're accompanied by any small children, be sure they understand that you can't just go round pulling flowers off plants and eating them without asking a grown-up first.

Growing under glass

Maybe you've inherited a greenhouse. Or perhaps you're wondering how to use the cloches you have left over from last year. Or you're not sure what you're supposed to do with your cold frame. Do you put these seedlings in the greenhouse or in a cold frame?

Quite frankly, proper heated greenhouse gardening is only for the truly dedicated; those past the point of needing to look up quick reference points in a book such as this. Everything inside the greenhouse is your responsibility: soil, water, temperature, light, air. All these need constant adjusting. And there's an army of pests that really appreciate the shelter and warmth so you have to fumigate regularly. You need to be there all the time to pull the blinds down when the day suddenly turns baking hot, or sprinkle the floor with water to increase humidity. If you're out at work or, worse still, on holiday, that could be disastrous.

Nevertheless, unheated greenhouses, cloches, cold frames and the like do have their uses for gardeners like us. But what precisely are their uses? Essentially, they all do basically the same job: they raise the soil and air temperature around the plants without depriving them of light (or water so long as you provide it) so as to protect them from cold and windy weather. The difference in how they are used is only a matter of size and flexibility.

Here's a quick rundown of each so if you have one, or are thinking of getting one, you'll know how to get the best from it. And if you have a tray of seedlings you're at a loss to know what to do with, you'll know where to put it.

∽ Unheated greenhouse (or glasshouse) ∽

This is relatively expensive, unless you have inherited it, and is of course not moveable. This means you need to bring in soil for it, and will need to feed the soil regularly or it will quickly lose its nutrients.

Uses

o Starting off tender ornamental plants.

o Starting off tender and hardy vegetables.

o Growing on tender vegetables which like heat such as *tomato, cucumber, pepper, aubergine*.

o Overwintering some tender plants.

Pros

o It gives you enough height for tall crops such as *tomatoes* and *cucumbers*.

o You can store resting indoor ornamental plants in it.

o It gives you a sheltered work area in bad weather.

Cons

o Unless you heat it, your greenhouse will probably be redundant in the winter except perhaps for a few over-wintering plants.

o You need to water plants in a greenhouse regularly, often twice a day in hot weather.

o Pests can be a particular problem in the shelter of a greenhouse.

Rule of thumb ✣

Always keep a full watering can or two in your greenhouse. It helps the humidity, and means it's always at the right temperature for watering.

∾ Fixed cold frame (or garden frame) ∾

A fixed cold frame is very stable but, obviously, fixed. This means that, for example, you can't use it to house cuttings if it's in the sun as they like shade, unless you use something like sacking to cover part of it. On the other hand it won't blow away in a gale.

Uses

o Raising early seed.

o Housing cuttings.

o Hardening off non-hardy plants.

o Overwintering tender plants.

o Growing plants later than you could outside its protection eg *lettuce*.

Pros

o Helps protect against birds and caterpillars.

o Usually more stable than a cloche and, if it's large enough, it may retain more heat.

o You can increase the protection in very cold weather by covering it with sacking at night.

Cons

o Less flexible than a cloche as you can't move it around.

o Cold frames can be almost airtight so you need to be careful that you provide the necessary ventilation.

∼ Cloche or moveable cold frame ∼

You need to keep these clean or you'll be blocking out the light. Glass is better than plastic for providing both light and heat, and is easier to keep clean (though if you have children who are fanatical cricket players plastic has a good deal to recommend it).

Uses

o Sowing seeds early.

o Warming the soil ready for planting in early spring.

o Drying out sodden soil before planting.

o Continuing growth in autumn after the first frosts for tender plants such as *lettuce* and *tomato*.

o Bringing on early *strawberries*.

Pros

o It's moveable so you can put it wherever you want it.

o You don't need to do much watering because rain runs off

the cloche into the soil alongside and will percolate through, but in very dry weather you'll need to water as well (you can put the hose at the side of the cloche without bothering to move it if you want).

o You can increase the protection in very cold weather by covering it with sacking at night.

Cons

o Cloches can be prone to blowing away in very blustery weather, so you need to fix them very firmly.

o Keep it clean or you're blocking out light – glass is better than plastic for both light and heat, and easiest to clean.

Rule of thumb ❧

Don't overcrowd plants under glass or you will encourage disease, especially fungal diseases.

Seasonal jobs for unheated greenhouses, cloches and frames

	Cold greenhouse	Fixed cold frame	Moveable cold frame/cloche
Spring	Thorough clean	Start *tomatoes, aubergines* etc in seed trays and pots	Warm up soil for early out-door sowings of *radish, let-tuce, corn salad, onions, car-rots*
	Dig and manure borders, or prepare growbags, for *tomatoes, cucumber, early herbs, salad crops* etc	Also start early flowering annuals eg *sweet pea, antirrhinum*	Protect late sowings of *broad beans, peas* for crop-ping early next year
	Start *tomatoes, aubergines* etc in seed trays and pots	Harden off plants sown indoors	Protect emerging plants in borders against late frosts eg *dahlia, lily*
	Also start early flowering annuals eg *sweet pea, antirrhinum*	Plant *tomatoes, cucumber, early herbs, salad crops* etc	Harden off plants sown indoors
	Prick out seedlings and grow on plants		Cover *strawberries* for earlier cropping

	Cold greenhouse	Fixed cold frame	Moveable cold frame/cloche
Summer	Grow on tender crops such as *tomatoes, cucumber, melon, pepper* etc Tie in *tomatoes* and pinch out side shoots Check regularly for pests and diseases Hand pollinate *melons, cucumbers* etc	Grow on tender crops such as *tomatoes, cucumber, melon, pepper* etc Use to put out tender plants initially, in pots eg *French bean, tomatoes*	Use to put out tender plants initially, in pots eg *French bean, tomatoes*
Autumn	Finish cropping *tomatoes* etc Late sowings of *lettuce, endive, corn salad, radish* Sow *sweet peas* for early flowering	Dry off *onions and shallots* Late sowings of *lettuce, endive, corn salad, radish*	Dry off *onions and shallots* Late sowings of *lettuce, endive, corn salad, radish*

Prepare areas to store plants which will not overwinter outside eg lifted *dahlia* tubers (store in dry sand), *argyranthemum 'Jamaican primrose'*, *geranium (pelargonium)*, *heliotrope*. If space is short, take cuttings and discard the larger plants Clean glass	Grow on tender crops such as *tomatoes*, *cucumber*, *melon*, *pepper* etc Use to put out tender plants initially, in pots eg *French bean*, *tomatoes*	Use to put out tender plants initially, in pots eg *French bean*, *tomatoes*
Winter Overwinter plants which need frost protection	Overwinter plants which need frost protection	Cover overwintering salad crops such as *mizuna, corn salad, claytonia*

You'll need to water cold greenhouses, cold frames and cloches, and keep them well ventilated, and shaded if necessary, throughout the year if you have plants growing in them.

Rule of thumb 🌿

Close doors, windows, vents and lids in windy weather.

∾ Conservatory ∾

In theory, you can heat your conservatory well enough to grow tropical plants in it. However, you'll end up sweltering in the humid heat, especially in the summer and it won't be comfortable to live in. Then again, you can compromise on this if you want to and you're passionate about tropical plants.

Broadly speaking, you can grow the same plants in your conservatory as you can elsewhere in the house, but they'll have more light and heat so they should grow better. You're also more likely to notice them than you would in a greenhouse so you'll remember to water, ventilate and shade them when necessary.

You can grow pretty much the same plants in a conservatory as you can in a cold greenhouse. If you're wondering which plants will enjoy being moved into your conservatory for the winter and will give you pleasure at the same time, here are some typical plants which would be suitable:

o *abutilon*

o *African violet*

o *calceolaria*

o *cineraria*

o *ferns*

o *geranium (pelargonium)*

o *heliotrope*

o *palms*

o *plumbago capensis*

o *primula sinensis*

o *schizanthus*

o some orchids such as *cymbidiums*

o forced bulbs such as *paper white narcissus, hyacinth, amaryllis*

Always keep a bowl of water in your conservatory to keep the humidity up.

Compost and waste

In gardening terms, the word 'compost' really isn't sufficient to describe the variety of materials you can use or purposes you can put them to, all falling under the general term 'compost'. What you want to know right now, however, is what you're supposed to be using and how. Or, if you make your own compost, a quick reminder of what you can and can't put on your compost heap.

It is possible to break down the meanings of the word into two main groups:

1 A mixture of different soils and nutrients you can buy in bags, usually for planting or growing things in.

2 Well rotted vegetable matter and/or farmyard manure which is more often applied to the soil or dug into it, and includes your own garden compost.

We'll look at each of these in turn.

∾ Soils and nutrients ∾

This kind of compost is the stuff you buy down at the garden centre. There are various different types, each one being a different mixture of soil components and nutrients designed for a specific purpose. They are sterile, so they should contain no diseases, pests or weeds. If you're wondering what kind you need, or debating with yourself whether it would be OK to use that leftover half bag in the shed to pot up your seedlings, here is a quick guide:

o *John Innes seed compost* is for sowing seeds.

o *John Innes cutting compost* is ideal for rooting cuttings.

o *John Innes potting compost no 1* is formulated for pricking out and potting up young seedlings and rooted cuttings.

o *John Innes potting compost no 2* is for general potting up and potting on of house plants and vegetables into medium sized pots.

o *John Innes potting compost no 3* is for final potting of hungry plants (such as tomatoes) and for trees and shrubs grown in containers.

Pocket facts

John Innes was a wealthy Victorian who died in 1904 leaving his fortune to horticultural research. The John Innes Horticultural Research Institute developed standardised recipes for composts for different purposes, which can be used by commercial companies in their own branded compost products.

o *Multipurpose compost* can be used for just about anything, as the name suggests. Obviously it's not likely to be as ideal for whatever you're potting at the moment as a more specific compost, but it will do the job.

o *Planting and potting compost* is, as the name suggests, suitable for planting and potting.

o *Seed compost* – yes, you guessed it – it's for planting seeds in.

o *Ericaceous compost* is designed for acid loving plants such as *rhododendron*, *camellia* or *heather* which won't otherwise grow in your soil because it's too alkaline. You can either plant these plants in the compost in a large pot or, when you plant, you can dig a hole and fill it with ericaceous compost to plant into, although this won't last for ever as worms and weather will inevitably mix up the soils. Ericaceous compost traditionally contains peat which is acid.

o *Growbags* are designed for you to plant straight into; you can put them on a patio, for instance, and grow tomatoes in them. All you do is slit the bag, make drainage holes and plant into it. Then water. They are designed for hungry plants but, even so, you may also have to feed greedy plants as the season wears on.

There are also some composts available down at the garden centre which are made specially for specific plants, such as tomato compost.

↭ Peat free gardening

Many gardeners, as lovers of nature and the outdoors, are concerned at the destruction of natural peat bogs and their resident wildlife. The fact is that peat bogs take thousands of years to form and are being dug up, largely for the benefit of us gardeners, at an alarming rate. If you don't want to be a part of this disturbing trend, you can now buy peat free varieties of many composts, though John Innes composts are not peat free. You'll also find organic composts on sale in larger garden centres.

∾ Rotted vegetable matter or ∾ farmyard manure

Again there are several varieties of these. If a neighbouring farmer has just offered you some chicken manure, or you're wondering whether to dig composted bark into your vegetable plot (the answer's no, by the way) here are a few clues:

o *Farmyard manure* is animal dung (from cows, horses, sheep or pigs) often mixed with straw, sawdust or shredded newspaper. It needs to be well rotted down as the acids in fresh manure are harmful to plants. It is excellent for digging into the soil to condition it but it can often contain weed seeds unless it's very well rotted, so it's not much good as a mulch. If you're my mother you'll keep carrier bags in the car and stop and leap out excitedly to scoop up any horse dung you spot on country lanes. This is (she tells me) well worth doing as it really is an excellent form of compost once it's well rotted down.

o *Chicken manure* is very strong and needs to be stored for several months (you can buy it pelleted and ready to use). Apparently it improves the flavour of raspberries considerably, so long as you don't think about it too hard while eating them. Add it to your compost heap as an activator if it's fresh.

o *Composted bark* contains little nutrient value but is a good improver of soil structure which means it helps the soil retain water, so it's good as a mulch. (Beware though of providing a good hiding place for slugs.) Woody materials take a lot of nitrogen from the soil when breaking down, so it's a good idea to sprinkle the area with bonemeal or blood, fish and bonemeal.

o *Spent mushroom compost* is a waste product of mushroom growing (no surprises there). The contents vary and usually include farmyard manure. It contains good nutrients and plenty of bulk so is good for digging into the soil, particularly in the brassica section of the vegetable garden. It also includes chalk so don't use it on plants that dislike lime, such as *meconopsis, gentian, rhododendron, potato*.

o *Seaweed* is a very good soil conditioner to dig in, containing plenty of nutrients including valuable trace elements.

o *Leaf mould* is very valuable for both nutrients and moisture retaining humus (so you can spread it around your plants in the autumn). You can't generally buy it but it's easy to make your own (see below). It lightens heavy soils, and helps light soils to retain moisture. It's very good for potting.

o *Garden compost* is what you make yourself in the garden out of vegetable waste (see below). Spread it around hungry plants such as *roses* and fruit bushes in the autumn to provide additional nutrients, and to dig into the soil, especially in the vegetable garden.

Pocket facts

Beech and oak leaves make the fastest, and among the best, leaf moulds if regularly turned.

↪ Leaf mould

If it's autumn and your garden is filling up with fallen leaves, don't despair: be happy. You have the ingredients for delicious home made leaf mould.

o Collect up all your dead leaves and pack them into black plastic sacks.

o Tie the top of the sack and push it down to form a hollow where rainwater can collect.

o Punch a few holes in the top of the sack so a little water can get in, and a few in the sides to let in insects and worms.

o Alternatively you can pile up the leaves in a mesh or wooden slatted, open top container such as you use for compost. This can take longer but the process will be speeded up if you add leaf mould accelerator, which you can buy at most garden centres.

o By next autumn your leaf mould should have rotted down ready to use.

✎ Garden compost

Not only does a compost heap enable you to make your own compost, it also gives you somewhere to put most of your garden waste. If you don't yet have a compost heap, it's a good idea to start one. Here's how to pick the right spot:

o It should be out of the wind, the heat of the sun and the worst of the rain.

o Site it where there is good air circulation around it.

o The base should be earth or rubble – nothing impermeable.

The compost heap must be able to heat up in order to kill weed seeds and decompose the material. So it should:

o be moist but not wet (a piece of old carpet over the top will keep out the worst of the rain), and o hold air so it mustn't be too squashed down

o have good air circulation so it needs to be made of slatted wood or some other material with plenty of air holes or spaces

The optimum size is around 3-4' square by the same sort of height. You can add compost activators which you can buy at the garden centre to speed up the process, or use a natural activator such as chicken manure. If you add nothing the process just takes a bit longer, that's all.

If you have two compost heaps it means you can be filling one up while the other matures, which is ideal. Otherwise you either have to leave your compost heap alone while it matures, or keep taking compost from the bottom as you fill it from the top. Best of all is three compost heaps. Here's how each one is used if you go for this option:

	Heap 1	*Heap 2*	*Heap 3*
Year 1	Filling	-	-
Year 2	Maturing	Filling	-
Year 3	Using	Maturing	Filling
Year 4	Filling	Using	Maturing
Year 5	Maturing	Filling	Using

Perhaps you're holding this book in one hand and a weed you've just pulled in the other. Or the teabag from the cup of tea you just earned yourself after all that digging. Can you put it on the compost heap? Here's a quick checklist of things you can and can't compost.

YES	NO
Any soft vegetable matter from the garden (other than virulent perennial weeds)	Hard woody stuff from the garden such as rose or tree prunings (unless you've put it through a fine shredder first)
Uncooked kitchen refuse such as vegetable peelings, tea leaves and teabags, outside leaves from *cabbage* etc	Virulent weeds such as *bindweed*, *couch grass* or *ground elder* (and don't talk to me about ground elder either)
Human urine – yes, peeing on your compost heap speeds up the decomposition process	Cooked food (which attracts rats, as well as being no good as compost)
Dung from herbivores such as horses, cows, chickens etc (OK so chickens aren't strictly herbivores, but their diet is generally plant based)	Cat or dog poo
Fresh bonfire ash	Coal ashes or cinders
Sawdust from untreated timber	Wood shavings
	Dead leaves, which are better made into leaf mould (see above). A few won't matter, but they take longer to rot down
	Anything that you think may be diseased

YES	NO
	Any animal matter, from kitchen waste meat to dead birds you failed to rescue from the cat in time (and it attracts rats)
	Leather

Turning a compost heap

You may have some vague idea that you're supposed to turn a compost heap. Quite so. The idea is that the material on the outside rots slower than the material in the hot centre. So it's only sensible to mix it all round and give all your compost a go in the middle. So when and how do you turn a compost heap?

o As for when, you should turn the heap a few weeks after you've finished adding material to it. By this time the heap should have shrunk to about a third of its original size.

o Dig all the compost out of the heap and pile it up nearby. Then put it all back again, mixing as you go and shaking out any compressed material.

o If you have room you can simply transfer the whole heap to a fresh location, mixing as you go.

What do you do with everything else?

o Woody matter, weeds and discarded material should all be burnt. If you live in an area where bonfires aren't allowed, bag it up and take it to the dump.

o Dead leaves can be made into leaf mould (see above).

o You can put thin layers of grass cuttings on the compost heap alternating with coarser material. But if you have large expanses of lawn you'll deluge the poor compost heap and it will turn into a slimy mass. The rest can be dumped in a designated pile somewhere and will eventually turn into compost (especially if a lot of your lawn isn't really grass anyway).

Warning

One final word before you start putting that compost on your garden: don't be impatient. If you spread the compost before it's ready, you'll be spreading weeds.

∽ Bonfires ∽

Before you light a bonfire you need to be sure that you're allowed to have bonfires; many parts of the country aren't, and are only permitted incinerators.

✎ What can you burn?

A lot of your garden waste goes on the compost heap, so what is it that should go on the bonfire?

o Woody material that won't go on the compost heap, eg shrub and tree prunings, old *cabbage* stumps, twiggy remains of perennials too tough to compost such as *Michaelmas daisy*.

o Any diseased material.

o Roots and stems of invasive plants that will reproduce if put on the compost heap, eg *bindweed, ground elder, enchanter's nightshade*.

⌖ *Dos and don'ts for bonfires*

o Do try to choose a windless day. If there's a bit of a breeze make sure it's not blowing towards a neighbour's washing line or favourite sitting area.

o Do make sure all the material is as dry as possible to create minimum smoke.

o Do make sure there's no wildlife in the danger zone such as hedgehogs or grass snakes before you light the bonfire. It's a good idea to make the fire a few feet away from the heap and fork across the waste material bit by bit.

o Don't ever put liquid fuel on the bonfire once it's alight. The flames can run up the path of the fuel to your hand.

o Do burn the most combustible material first, and the rest after the fire has got a good hold.

o Do make sure the fire doesn't get too compacted or it will go out because of lack of oxygen. Lift and loosen it with a garden fork to re-aerate.

o Do make sure the flames are extinguished and the bonfire is safely out before you leave it.

o Don't throw the ash away. It's a good source of potash and can go either on the compost heap or straight on the garden once it's cold.

Rule of thumb ❧

5 November is a good day for a bonfire. It's hard for any neighbours to object, and you should have done your autumn cutback.

Garden structure

The walls, fences, pond or lawn in your garden are as much a part of it as the flowers. These structural features don't usually need as much attention as the growing plants – assuming they're reasonably sound and not close to collapse – but there are still some on-the-spot tasks which are worth a quick reminder. So here's a run through of the key structural features of most gardens.

∾ Hedges ∾

As boundaries go, hedges take more work than most. You don't often need to attend to walls and fences, but hedges will need some input from you. Before you take the trimmer to your overgrown hedge, here's a quick guide to the main types of hedging giving planting distances and any other notes on maintenance.

↬ Evergreen hedging

This gives a good windbreak in the winter when it's most needed. The denser the growth, the better the plant is for topiary. Be aware that some evergreens will sprout copiously if you cut them hard back, while others will never reshoot if you cut back beyond the green parts.

	Planting distance	*Comments*
Box	6-9" (15-23cm)	Good for edging and knot gardens, needs regular cutting. Don't cut back beyond the green growth.
Cypress	30" (75cm)	Includes Leylandii. Grows fast and very high, and won't reshoot if you cut it back beyond the green. So don't let it get out of hand.
Holly	24" (60cm)	Slow growing and, obviously, prickly. Reshoots when cut hard back.
Laurel	4' (1.2m)	Various types. You can cut this back hard if you need to.
Privet	15" (35cm)	Very hungry – if you have trouble growing anything near it, that's why. Fast growing and may need trimming more than once a year.
Yew	24" (60cm)	Slow growing. Reshoots well however hard you cut it back.

✦ *Deciduous hedging*

You can prune a hedge at any time of year in theory, but if you're growing a deciduous hedge which keeps its leaves in winter, such as beech, prune it in August so it can put out new leaves which will still be firmly anchored through winter. Earlier leaves will fall in autumn.

	Planting distance	Comments
Beech	24" (60cm)	Keeps its copper-brown leaves all winter after a late prune.
Hawthorn	12" (30cm)	Easy and fast growing. And thorny, of course.
Hornbeam	24" (60cm)	Keeps its leaves all winter after a late prune. Good on light, dry soil.

⤳ Ornamental hedging

You should trim ornamental hedges after flowering, although if they have berries you'll lose a lot of these. Then again, if you wait to trim until the berries are gone in early spring you risk losing some of next year's flowers. Your call.

	Planting distance	Comments
Berberis	18" (45cm)	Prickly and needs little trimming
Cotoneaster	21" (50cm) (60-75cm)	Attractive berries which you'll lose if you trim after flowering.
Escallonia	24-30"	Useful in coastal gardens as well as good elsewhere

Pyracantha	24" (60cm)	Tough and hardy. Attractive berries which you'll lose if you trim after flowering.
Rose	2' (60cm)	Some varieties are good for hedging. They can be pruned with hedge trimmers.

Rule of thumb 🐛

Don't cut hedges between March and the end of July as you may disturb nesting birds which will abandon their nests.

♔ Pruning a new hedge

The more often you trim the sides of a young hedge the better. The idea is to encourage it to keep sprouting until it has a thicket of twigs. Just make sure you don't cut it back beyond the green if it's a variety that won't reshoot. Leave the top to grow until it has reached the height you want.

♔ Pruning an overgrown hedge

If you have inherited a hedge which is completely overgrown (obviously you wouldn't have let it get that way yourself) you need to cut it back hard to get rid of the straggly, bare growth and to reduce its size. The time and method for doing this depends on the type of hedge:

o *Deciduous* Prune these hard in late February while they are still dormant. To keep the hedge looking thicker, prune one side of the hedge one year and the other side the following year.

o *Evergreen* (excluding conifers and box) Prune hard in late March. Again, prune one side of the hedge one year, the other the next.

o *Conifers and box* Since these can't be cut back hard, you'll need to dig them out and replant the hedge. If you're using box as an edging plant, you can take cuttings and use them to fill gaps in the hedge, replacing the worst sections each year, rather than grub up the whole hedge.

o *Lavender and rosemary* These both make excellent low hedging plants. If they become straggly they will need replacing, but take cuttings first. Within a few months you'll be able to replace the hedge with its own cuttings.

✧ *Before you get the hedge trimmer out...*

If you haven't done any hedge trimming for a year, or maybe the hedge trimmer is a new acquisition, it's worth a quick recap of the top half dozen safety guidelines for using an electric trimmer:

1 Use an RCD (circuit breaker) at the electric socket.

2 Drape the lead over your shoulder so it can't get in the way of the blades.

3 Wear goggles to protect your eyes from flying twigs and leaves.

4 Make sure there's nothing in the hedge that could catch on the blades.

5 Don't stretch to reach a section of hedge. Move closer, if necessary moving the ladder or whatever you're standing on more frequently.

6 Don't try to slice your way through thick branches. Come back later with a set of loppers.

And remember to spread out a sheet of some kind under the hedge to catch the trimmings – it makes the tidying up much easier.

∼ Walls ∼

Walls can support climbers and trained shrubs that even fences can't, which makes them ideal for growing your favourite plants. If you have a new plant in your hand and can't decide which wall to plant it against, it makes a big difference which way the wall faces. A south facing wall (ie the wall on the northern boundary of your garden) will get lots of sunshine and will suit any climbers except those which want cool shade. A north facing wall, by contrast, will get no sun and won't suit sun loving plants at all.

Here's a table of which common climbing plants and wall shrubs will grow on or against each type of wall. Obviously this assumes that there are no other factors affecting the wall. If your south facing wall has a huge tree with dense foliage a few feet in front of it, the wall won't be as sunny as a typical south facing wall.

South facing	West facing	North facing	East facing
Gets lots of sunshine and is hot and drier than other walls	Starts the day chilly but gets the sun later when it is at its warmest	No sun, so may not lose the frost all day in winter. Most likely wall to be damp	Gets the morning sun, but is in shade for much of the rest of the day
Almost anything except camellias, honeysuckle (unless the ground is damp) and clematis (unless its roots are in the shade). Especially good for: *actinidia kolomikta, ceanothus, cobaea scandens, cotoneaster, morning glory, passion flower, peach, solanum crispum, sweet pea, variegated ivy, wisteria*	*apricot, clematis honeysuckle, pear rose, solanum crispum, vine*	*camellia, cotoneaster, forsythia,* some clematis (eg *'Miss Bateman', tangutica*) some roses (eg *'Zephyrine Drouhin'*) *winter jasmine* plus all the climbers on p114 which will grow anywhere	Much the same as for north facing, but not good for *camellias,* or tender plants which can't cope with morning sun after a frost.

Some climbers will co-operatively thrive just about anywhere, so long as the soil isn't too dry or too sodden. Here
are the most typical examples:

akebia quinata   *hydrangea petiolaris*   *Russian vine*
clematis montana   *ivy*   *summer jasmine*
clematis tangutica   *pyracantha*   *Virginia creeper*

Rule of thumb

*Flower beds at the base of high walls may need extra water-
ing as they can be dry and overprotected from the rain. Put
new plants at least 12" (30cm) away from the wall.*

↬ Ivy and walls

There's often a confusion about whether ivy is good or bad
for walls. The reason it's hard to get a consistent answer on
this is because there isn't one: it depends on the wall. If the
mortar in the wall is a modern impermeable mix, the ivy
will do it no harm as it won't be able to penetrate the wall
itself. However, ivy can bring down an old wall built using
lime mortar (it's happened to me), because it can burrow
right into the mortar. As the stems grow and expand, they
can force the bricks or stones apart.

↬ Repairing walls with climbers on them

Not a lot of fun this. But for guidelines on how to go about
it, see fences (below).

～ Fences ～

The only routine maintenance your fence is likely to need
is a coat of preservative every few years. If it starts to fall

apart or rot you may need to replace some or all of it. So the only thing you're likely to need to know right now, is what to do with your climbing plants while you work on the fence.

o Carefully work along the fence undoing any ties attaching the plant to the fence.

o Lay the plant flat on the ground – that's what all the books say but, of course, there are probably loads of other plants in the way. So just lay it as flat as you can so that it's supported. Leave yourself access to paint the fence (or whatever you're doing) without treading on the climbers.

o The standard advice if you're replacing the fence is to work from the other side. However, for most of us this requires a very understanding neighbour. If you can do it, however, you should now erect the fence from the other side.

o When you have finished work, tie your climbers back in again.

If you want to know what plants will grow against fences of different orientations, it's the same as for walls (above).

∼ Climbing structures ∼

There are plenty of other ways of growing plants vertically. If you're wondering whether your pergola will suit a particular plant, or whether this year's sweet peas will work over an arch, here's a quick rundown of the main types of structure and what plants you can grow up them.

↬ Pergola

This is a series of archways straddling a path. For planting purposes a gazebo or bower comes to the same thing. You need to plant your climbers one at the bottom of each post so they can scramble up and over the top to give shade and, often, scent. Suitable flowering climbers for pergolas include:

clematis	rose (climbing or rambling)
honeysuckle	sweet pea
laburnum	wisteria

Suitable crops to grow up pergolas include:

cucumber	runner bean
grapevine	squash
marrow	

↬ Arch

These are similar in height and structure to pergolas, but with less space so you need only one climber each side. This means that less vigorous plants are better suited to arches, for example *rambling* rather than *climbing roses*.

↬ Pillar

Whether it's an elegant wrought iron pillar or an old post or stump, it comes to the same thing when you're choosing what to plant. You need to grow climbers which aren't too vigorous or they'll quickly outgrow the pillar. If you have any of the following, this could be a good spot for them:

less vigorous variety of clematis	nasturtium
less vigorous variety of honeysuckle	rambling rose
morning glory	sweet pea

✥ Wigwam

This can vary from a home made wigwam of bamboo poles to an iron obelisk. These tend to be relatively short, about 4-6', and of course there's less room for climbers at the top because of the shape. Wigwams are best for low growing plants and are often used when several plants are planted around the base. They are good for annual plants. Good choices for wigwams include:

black-eyed susan   *nasturtium*
non-vigorous clematis (eg alpina)   *runner bean*
morning glory   *sweet pea*

Rule of thumb ❧

When you're deciding where to plant a climber, always consider three factors:
o *space (width and height)*
o *aspect (which way does it face)*
o *sun and shade levels*

∾ Lawns ∾

Some of us like perfect green lawns with no trace of any plant but grass, while others of us are happy with little better than a mown field. This section is chiefly about how to achieve the former – you can use as much of it as you need according to where on the bowling green/tussocky field scale you are.

✥ Laying a lawn or new section of lawn

Have you got a worn patch of grass that would be better if you start again from scratch? Or have you decided to add a new area of lawn in part of your garden? The first thing is to choose whether you're going to use seed or turf. Here are the chief pros and cons:

Grass seed	Turf
Slower growing and you need to keep off it for longer	Instant grass, though you need to keep off it for a while for it to establish
Quicker and easier to sow	Slower and trickier to lay
Cheaper	More expensive
Better for filling in patches	

✤ Sowing a lawn from seed

Make sure you read the packet and use the right kind of seed. Cheap grass seed is rarely a good idea for lawns. You need to sow grass during the growing season. September is the best month, when the soil is warm and not too wet. If this is a very cold, wet September, or excessively dry, wait until the end of next March to sow the grass.

1 Ideally you should dig the soil over at least a month before sowing so the soil can settle. If you were planning to sow the seed today and haven't done this, try to do it now and wait at least a few days to sow the seed or you risk an uneven lawn. Alternatively – if you don't want to wait – you can rake, tread down, roll and water the soil to see where it's uneven. Then rake up and down and diagonally, treading it down again, to get it even.

2 A week before you sow the seed (ha! caught you out again!) apply lawn fertiliser, rake and firm the soil by walking over it repeatedly.

3 Sow the seed on a day when the soil is dry, distributing the seed as evenly as possible, at $1^1/2$oz per square yard (40g per square metre). Don't do this on a windy day.

4 Rake the ground lightly after sowing.

5 Leave the grass until it's 2-3" high before mowing on a high cut, and rolling if necessary.

✎ Laying a turf lawn

You can lay turf at any time of year except when it's frosty or very dry. October is a good month. You want turfs which are about 2" thick, and you need to lay them as soon as possible after delivery.

1 Follow steps 1 and 2 above for sowing grass seed.

2 Lay the turves by fitting them together, not too tightly, so that each row just slightly overlaps the previous one. Lay the turves in a brickwork pattern so that the joints don't line up across the rows.

3 If there is any unevenness in the surface, correct it by adding or removing soil underneath. Fill any gaps with fine soil (there shouldn't really be any, but we're all human).

4 Tread down well by laying down a plank and walking on it to prevent damaging the new turf.

5 Water the new lawn or the turves will shrink and leave gaps.

6 After a week or so you can mow it on a high setting.

7 Keep watering it regularly if the weather is dry.

Pocket facts

The air in the UK is apparently full of grass seed. What's more, grass is one of the few plants that thrives on having its head regularly cut off. This means that it is possible to make a perfectly acceptable lawn without seed or turf but simply by mowing an area regularly. The grass seed in the air will settle, and everything else will be killed or weakened by the mowing. It does take a long time, mind you.

✧ *Lawn maintenance*

If you want a perfect lawn, you have to work at it. If not, the occasional mow will probably do. Here's a rundown of the main jobs you need to do if you want to keep your lawn looking good. If it's looking a bit rough at the moment, this may give you a clue as to why, and how to remedy it.

o *Mow* Don't cut grass too short or you encourage moss. It's better to mow little and often. And change your mowing pattern occasionally. You can set aside areas which you delay mowing in spring so you can naturalise bulbs and grow early wild flowers. In this case, don't mow until the flowers have set seed and the leaves of the bulbs have died down.

o *Water* There's no point in watering lightly as it won't make any difference. If you're going to water your lawn in dry weather, do it thoroughly.

o *Rake and aerate* In March and October you should use a wire rake to rake and aerate the lawn, and remove moss. Scarify the lawn by rolling it with a spiked roller, piercing it all over with a garden fork, or raking with a spring toothed rake in October.

o *Sweep* Don't leave autumn leaves to decay on the lawn.

o *Weed* Hand weed large tap rooted weeds such as *dandelion* and *dock*. Or apply a spot weedkiller to each one individually. You can put selective weedkillers on a lawn but this means you'll kill off any *daisies* and wild flowers in your lawn which may not be what you want to do.

o *Feed* Grass needs potash and phosphates in the autumn, and nitrogen in spring, to grow lush and healthy. Apply the potash and phosphates in November and the nitrogen in March, following the instructions on the packet.

⌁ Dry weather

In hot dry weather, your lawn may develop cracks if the soil is quite high in clay. Brush sand into the cracks to improve the look of the lawn and help drainage. Mow on a higher cut in dry spells, too, to prevent the lawn turning brown.

Pocket facts

It's reckoned to be winter when the temperature drops below 6°C (42°F). The reason behind this seemingly random figure is that this is the temperature below which grass stops growing. The number of winter days each year varies widely according to where in the UK you are. In the very far south west there is an average of no more than 30 days of winter all year (hardly worth putting the lawn mower away). Obviously these won't necessarily be consecutive days. In parts of the country such as the Pennines and the Scottish highlands, most years see more than 140 days of winter, nearly 5 months.

∾ Ponds ∾

If you have a pond in your garden, you probably won't need to spend a lot of time working on it. However, there are a few problems which arise with ponds which you may want the solution to.

✧ Blanket weed

If your pond starts to cover over with algae or blanket weed, float a bundle of barley straw in it. (No idea why this works, before you ask.)

✧ Evaporation

Top up your pond with rainwater rather than tap water, to avoid introducing the minerals in tap water which can encourage weeds.

✧ Weeding

If you're weeding your pond, leave the weeds on the edge of the pond for a while before composting them so any small creatures can escape and crawl back into the water.

✧ Ice

If your pond ices up heavily in the winter and you keep fish in it you need to make holes in the ice. However you shouldn't hit the ice or the shock waves may harm the wildlife in the pond. Fill a container with hot water and stand it on the ice until it melts a hole through it. If you don't keep fish in your pond, the wildlife should survive happily as only the very shallowest ponds will freeze solid, though you'll need to put out fresh water for the birds.

Moving water is much less likely to freeze. You'll normally need to turn off any fountains in very cold weather, but you can still keep the surface of your pond moving to reduce the risk of icing over. Float a few beachballs on it, which will be blown by the wind to keep the movement going. Better still, encourage ducks and moorhens to swim in your pond.

Wildlife gardening

One of the joys of gardening is that it gives you the chance to watch and hear the birds, insects and other wildlife. The excitement of finding a hidden nest, or turning over a stone to uncover a millipede or stag beetle, is a huge part of the pleasure. So this section is all about how to bring the widest variety of wildlife into your garden. Look, I confess this is less of an on-the-spot subject than some of the earlier sections, but wildlife is critical in the garden and it's often when you've just seen it while you're working in the garden that you think of looking up how to make sure it stays around.

If you want to encourage butterflies, or you've just seen a slow worm and want to know how to attract more of them, the answer should be here. The first part of this section is arranged according to the wildlife you want to bring into your garden. Many of these creatures are very beneficial to the garden; toads, for example, are as good a method of slug control as you'll find anywhere. I haven't included wildlife which is detrimental to the garden: however much you like rabbits, deer or badgers, the chances are you won't actually want them among your flowers or vegetables.

∼ Bats ∼

There are two things which will attract bats to your garden: suitable roosts, and plenty of night flying insects for food.

o *Bat roosts* As well as organising bat boxes and so on (your local Wildlife Trust can direct you to a bat conservation group for advice) the most useful way to garden for bats is to leave old and dying trees in the garden rather than destroying them, as they may well contain cavities which bats will want to roost in.

o *Food for bats* The best ways to attract night flying insects for bats are to have a pond (even a small one), or a wild flower area which will have numerous insects living among the grasses. If you have – or want – bats, never spray insecticides as bats eat hundreds of insects a night.

∾ Bees, hoverflies and other ∾ beneficial insects

Bees are among the most beneficial insects of all – honey bees, bumble bees and others. They pollinate flowers and crops, trees and shrubs. One of the best ways to attract them is with their favourite nectar flowers. The following flowers all attract insects, especially bees:

bluebell	*foxglove*	*rosemary*
broom	*hyssop*	*snapdragon*
clover	*lavender*	*sunflower*
flowering currant	*poached egg plant*	*thyme*

Hoverflies particularly like *pussy willow, marigold* and *salad burnet*.

The best way to control pests is to let nature do it for you. If you provide a friendly habitat for hoverflies, ladybirds, lacewing flies, ground beetles and wasps (yes, wasps), they'll eat up your aphids, unwelcome caterpillars, sawflies and other pests. Here are the best ways to attract them:

o Beetles and other ground living insects like long grass, so it's worth keeping a small patch of unmown grass. Leave small stones and pieces of wood on the ground for day-time hiding places.

o Ladybirds hibernate in dry crevices or on leaves and stems of dead herbaceous perennials, so leave some untidied up until early spring.

o If you're burning prunings and debris, shake out the stems first to dislodge any ladybirds.

o Hoverflies love nectar, especially *carrot flowers*, so try to let the odd carrot go to seed as well as providing other nectar.

Rule of thumb 🐝

If you want to garden in as wildlife friendly a way as possible, never spray.

∽ Birds ∽

There's far more to attracting birds to your garden than simply having a bird table, though that undoubtedly helps. The three main things you need to provide to encourage birds into your garden are food, water and places to nest and roost. Here is a quick tour of your garden and how best to make each area friendly to birds.

↭ Hedges

Mixed hedges of native plants provide the most insect food for birds, and evergreen hedges give the best protection for nesting. A mixed hedge is best of all. Here are a few more ways to make your hedges as bird friendly as possible:

o Let a few plants in the hedge grow without trimming so they can fruit as food for the birds, for example *hawthorn, crab apple, privet*.

o If you have more than one hedge try to vary them, making one taller, wider or denser than another, and varying the hedging plants if you can, to attract a wider variety of birds.

o Never cut hedges between March and the end of July in case you disturb nesting birds.

✑ Walls and fences

Climbers, trees and shrubs trained against walls and fences give good cover for birds to nest. Here are some good examples:

o Plants which grow abundantly such as *summer jasmine* and *honeysuckle* make popular nest sites.

o Wall-trained plants such as *cotoneaster, japonica* and *pyracantha* also provide winter berries for the birds.

o *Ivy* is very popular because it's evergreen so the cover stays through the winter. It's very popular with wrens and robins (and also overwintering brimstone butterflies).

o *Wisteria* trained against a wall may attract spotted flycatchers if you're lucky.

Holes in walls make great nest sites for starlings, tits and wrens. So if you're repointing an old wall, leave a few holes for the birds (and bats may use them too).

✑ Trees

Trees provide vital lookout perches and song posts for birds, as well as nesting sites and food. It's a good idea to have at least one decent sized tree in your garden as a song post for blackbirds and thrushes. If you're thinking of getting rid of any trees in your garden, consider the birds, especially if the tree is native (non-native trees support many fewer species of insects for the birds to feed on). The more insect species a tree supports, the better it is for the birds. Here's the top of the league table.

Tree	Number of insects it can support
Oak	284
Willow	266
Birch	229
Hawthorn	149
Blackthorn	109
Poplar (including aspen)	97
Crab apple	93
Scots pine	91

✧ Providing water

Whether or not you have a pond, a bird bath is always a good idea, and especially so when there's no other water in the garden. Birds need to bathe as well as drink so whatever you provide should have sloping sides so they can easily get in and out.

✧ Feeding the birds

Some birds eat only seeds and fruit while others eat only insects, snails and worms. Many birds, however, will eat either according to what's available.

You can boost the levels of food in your garden by feeding

the birds from a bird table or some kind of feeder. Some birds prefer to feed on the ground so you can put food out for them there too. If you feed your garden birds they will become dependent on you, so it's important to be consistent and keep feeding all year round. Make sure all your feeding stations are sited out in the open, well away from shrubs or buildings where predators such as cats may lurk.

The other way to feed your birds is by growing plants which provide food for them. Here are some of their favourites:

Fruits and berries

apple	mistletoe
blackberry	pear
cotoneaster	plum
elderberry	privet
hawthorn	pyracantha
holly	rose
ivy	rowan

Seeds, nuts and cones

acorn	groundsel
alder	knapweed
chickweed	larch
clover	most annual weeds
corn	sunflower
dandelion	thistle
grasses	

As with all wildlife, you can attract birds by making sure you don't tidy up too much. A few weeds left to seed, a dead branch left where it fell, a pile of cut grass here, a log pile or heap of stones there – they all get used by wildlife. A lot of insects and seeds means a lot of birds.

If you want to attract raptors such as owls and kestrels, a pond or wild flower area with long grasses provides cover to attract their prey species of mice, voles and shrews.

∽ Butterflies and moths ∽

These insects have two totally different phases – the caterpillar and the adult – so you need to make sure your garden is friendly to both. Generally speaking, here are the best ways to attract a good variety of butterflies and moths to your garden:

o Supply water in dry weather – a bird bath or a saucer of water.

o Grow plenty of nectar rich flowers for them to feed on.

o Butterflies like sun but dislike wind, so grow their favourite plants in a sunny, sheltered spot.

o Some butterflies hibernate in *ivy* and evergreens so try not to clear away all your ivy. Some prefer dead leaves on plants, so save some of your autumn tidying up and cutting back until spring.

o Leave windfall *apples, pears* and *plums* as many butterflies will love them.

o Leave a shed window or door ajar to let hibernating butterflies in and out.

o Leave a patch of *nettles* in a sunny corner for butterflies to lay eggs on. They will only lay on young shoots though, so you can cut back the old *nettles* in late summer to promote new growth for autumn.

↭ Nectar sources for adults

Butterflies can emerge as early as February, and some species are still on the wing in November if the weather is mild. So you need to grow a range of good nectar plants which will provide food early and late in the season, as well as in between. Here are some of the best garden plants for nectar. As you'll see, many of them are wild flowers; if you can keep just a corner of your garden for wild flowers you'll be rewarded with a mass of butterflies. If you want plenty of butterflies try to grow at least a few from each group.

Nectar sources for butterflies

Early	Mid-season	Late
anemone blanda	knapweed	bramble (flower and
dandelion	lavender	fruit)
forget-me-not	lemon balm	buddleia
hyacinth	marjoram	goldenrod
primrose	mint	Michaelmas daisy
pussy willow	perennial	scabious
scilla	wallflower	sedum
	teasel	sunflower
	thistle	
	valerian	

Moths are attracted to many of the same plants as butterflies, but they have their own particular favourites.

Nectar sources for moths

Day flying moths	Night flying moths
buddleia	buddleia
scabious	honeysuckle

valerian	*periwinkle*
white campion	*petunia*
	privet
	tobacco plant
	verbena

✧ Food plants for caterpillars

The variety of plants that caterpillars feed on is enormous, and some are only food for one or two species. However there are one or two plants which are host to several species and are therefore well worth cultivating (and not spraying).

Nettles

comma	red admiral
painted lady	small tortoiseshell
peacock	

Wood violets

dark green fritillary	queen of Spain fritillary
high brown	silver washed fritillary
pearl-bordered fritillary	small pearl-bordered fritillary

Larger varieties of native grasses

marbled white	skipper
meadow brown	small heath

Pocket facts

The first butterfly of the year is the brimstone, a beautiful primrose yellow butterfly which can appear as early as February. If you want to attract it you'll need to grow buckthorn for its caterpillars.

∿ Dragonflies and damselflies ∿

These both eat insects but are so beautiful they are entirely excused being useful as well. You (or a close neighbour) need a pond to attract dragonflies and damselflies, although you may attract dragonflies from a nearby pond or river; damselflies won't stray so far from the water. Your pond should have:

o *Weed* for laying eggs on and as a habitat for the nymphs that hatch from the eggs.

o *Tall grasses, sedges* or *rushes* for the nymphs to climb up when they're ready to hatch, shed their skins and dry their wings.

o *Lush marginal planting* to provide a habitat for the smaller insects that dragonflies and damselflies feed on.

Wild flower areas will also attract dragonflies since they are good hunting grounds.

∿ Frogs, toads and newts ∿

These all eat slugs, snails, insects and worms (so you can harm them if you use insecticides or slug pellets). If you want these creatures in your garden you'll need a pond of some kind, and places for them to hide and hibernate.

o *Pond* This doesn't need to be very large at all. They need the pond to breed and spawn in, and they have different requirements: frogs like shallow water (about 4"/10cm), and toads and newts prefer deeper water. If your pond provides both you'll attract them all. You'll need plenty of weeds and marginal plants in the pond, to give cover to spawn, emerging tadpoles and young frogs, newts and toads. This will also house food species such as grasshoppers and spiders for the mature animals to feed on. Frogs may hibernate in the mud at the bottom of the pond (so don't treat the water with chemicals).

o *Hiding and hibernation* Toads, newts and some frogs hibernate on land. They also like to hide during the day in similar places, so you need to provide them with piles of stones, rotting logs, broken flowerpots and crevices in walls. Toads in particular can happily live in surprisingly dry places. You may find any of them in your compost heap (so be careful when turning it), or your bonfire pile (so take care when lighting it).

∽ Grass snakes ∽

These harmless snakes are very beautiful and a real treat to have in your garden. They eat only live prey such as mice, shrews, voles and frogs. You can help them by providing a pond, warmth, and plenty of nooks and crannies.

o *Pond* Grass snakes hunt in water – they are excellent swimmers – and will often choose habitats where there is a pond, especially if it has lush marginal planting which will contain frogs and other small creatures.

o *Warmth* A stone path, or simply a flat stone, in a sunny part of the garden will give your grass snake somewhere to bask. It will also choose to lay its eggs somewhere warm such as a compost heap, manure pile or heap of grass clippings, so provide what you can.

o *Nooks and crannies* Grass snakes hibernate in tree roots and wall crevices, so don't repoint every crack in the wall and clear away piles of stones.

Pocket facts

The easiest way to distinguish between the harmless grass snake and the poisonous adder is that a grass snake has a yellow band around the back of its neck, and an adder's diamond markings are so clear and distinct that there shouldn't be any doubt. Grass snakes do have markings but they are less distinct. Broadly speaking, if in doubt, it's probably a grass snake (adders are quite rare) and the yellow band will confirm it. But keep clear unless you're absolutely certain.

∾ Hedgehogs ∾

Hedgehogs eat loads of pests including slugs, snails, caterpillars, insects and beetles. You can provide them with foraging areas, food, protection and hibernation areas.

o *Foraging areas* Leaf litter and log piles make great foraging for hedgehogs, so leave these around in the corner of your garden. Don't use insecticides or slug pellets as hedgehogs eat so many insects and molluscs that they can easily be killed from a build up of poison. The hedgehog is at least as effective as the slug pellets anyway.

o *Food* In dry weather, especially in late summer when they need to build up fat reserves for the winter, you can help by putting out food for your hedgehog. Give them water (not milk) if there isn't a ready natural source, and leave out tinned dog or cat food (this doesn't work so well if you have dogs or cats).

o *Protection* The two biggest dangers for hedgehogs in the garden are ponds and bonfires. Make sure your pond has an easy way out for them, if necessary by creating a ramp from a long stone at an angle, or a plank weighted down at one end. If you have a cattle grid the same thing applies. The danger with bonfires is that you'll set light to your bonfire pile not realising there's a hedgehog in it. So always keep your bonfire pile next to the fire pit, and transfer it only when you're ready to light it.

o *Hibernation areas* Winter is the time hedgehogs are at greatest risk from cold, damage to their nests, flood or fire. Leave piles of leaves undisturbed in corners, behind sheds or under hedges for them through the winter.

Pocket facts

If you have badgers you won't get hedgehogs. They don't share territories as they eat a very similar diet. Also, badgers will kill and eat hedgehogs (they roll on them to make them open out).

∾ Slow worms ∾

Slow worms love slugs, as well as insects, spiders and other small creatures. Despite their name they are not slow at all, and can move extremely fast. If you want to encourage slow worms, give them warmth, and good cover (and a ready supply of slugs).

o *Warmth* Slow worms love a warm spot where they can stay hidden – something metal to soak up the heat, such as an old garden spade or some corrugated metal, leant up against a sunny wall. They will lay their eggs in a warm place such as the compost heap, pile of rotting manure or a heap of grass clippings, so make sure there's a suitable spot for them.

o *Good cover* Slow worms are predated on by kestrels and crows, so although they like to bask in the sun they need good camouflage or a quick escape route. Rather than a flat sunny stone, they will choose a pile of logs, a wall with plenty of crevices to escape into or a pile of stones. They also like sunny banks where they can hide in the long grass.

Rule of thumb

If you want plenty of wildlife in your garden, don't use chemicals of any kind. If they don't harm the beneficial wildlife directly, they will probably reduce its natural food supply. Far better to have toads and no slugs, than slug pellets and no slugs or toads.

∾ Natural pest control ∾

Wildlife gardening isn't compatible with spraying insecticides or putting down slug pellets. So how do you get rid of the pests? The answer is that with no chemicals, the garden has every chance of being rich in natural predators. Here are some of the worst pests, and the top predators to encourage if you want to control them naturally.

Pest	Predators
Aphids	Birds (eg tits)
	Hoverfly
	Lacewing fly
	Ladybird
Whitefly	Birds (eg tits)
	Hedgehog

	Ichneumon fly Wasps (common, solitary and parasitic)
Snails	Frog Ground beetle Thrush Toad
Slugs	Frog Ground beetle Hedgehog Slow worm Toad

See also plants to deter pests in the Troubleshooting section, on page 146.

～ Six wild flowers not to weed up ～

There are several wild flowers that you might regard as weeds in your garden, but which do a useful job in attracting wildlife:

o *Lady's smock or cuckoo flower* The food plant of the orange tip butterfly.

o *Primrose* An early source of nectar for bees and butterflies.

o *Foxglove* Bees and other insects love them.

o *Snowdrop* Provides an early feast for bees.

o *Honeysuckle* Moths love it.

o *Cowslip* Attracts long tongued insects such as bees and moths.

∽ Twelve dos and don'ts to encourage ∽ wildlife in your garden

1   Do leave flower seeds and hedge fruits until February before tidying or trimming.

2   Do provide shelter and cover for roosting and nesting sites.

3   Do provide supplementary food for birds and hedge-hogs.

4   Do provide water – a pond if you can but at least a bird bath.

5   Do leave untidy corners and piles of leaves, logs and stones for hedgehogs, reptiles and amphibians.

6   Do grow native plants.

7   Do set aside what space you can, even if it's only small, for wild flowers to attract insects and provide cover for small animals.

8   Do grow flowers which have nectar or seeds for birds and insects.

9   Don't cut hedges between March and the end of July, in order to leave nesting birds undisturbed.

10 Don't put fish in your pond if you want other wildlife (such as dragonflies, water beetles, tadpoles) as the fish will eat them.

11 Don't keep cats (I was told to include that on the list, but I want it known that I do so reluctantly).

12 Don't use pesticides, insecticides or slug pellets.

Troubleshooting

No matter how lovingly you tend your plants, there will be times when they get sick. Well looked after plants are healthier than those which are undernourished or in poor condition but, like people, even the most fit and robust occasionally suffer.

Pests and diseases affect the best tended gardens, and some plants are more vulnerable than others. Newer, highly bred varieties of flowers, fruit and vegetable are often more susceptible than the old fashioned varieties, which have survived for centuries because they are tough and easy to grow, though some new varieties have been bred specially to resist a particular disease.

Rule of thumb 🌿

If you spray chemical insecticides you may leave a residue that weakens other plants, so it's better to encourage as many beneficial insects and birds as you can to take care of the pests for you.

∼ Pests ∼

You'll find that if you spray a general insecticide to kill your greenfly, for example, it will also kill all the ladybird and hoverfly larvae which feed on greenfly. Since these insects take longer to regenerate that the aphids do, it's not hard to see that you're setting up an unnecessary problem for yourself. Far better to attract more beneficial insects in the first place (see page 125).

Another way to reduce pests is not to plant in large blocks. A mass of plants of the same type is the equivalent of holding up a large flag for garden pests with 'over here' written on it in big letters. Mix varieties of plants together and it will help to keep the pest problem to a minimum.

You can use biological controls to get rid of your pests for you. These are insects or other organisms that will eat the pest for you. You generally need to buy a specific control for a specific pest; you can find them in some large garden centres or buy them by mail order. Obviously, once all the pests are eaten the control will starve so you'll have to buy more if you get a fresh outbreak.

Pocket facts

One of the best mail order sources of biological controls, as well as plenty of other organic gardening supplies, is *The Organic Gardening Catalogue* (01932 253666 or www.organiccatalog.com).

✎ Slugs and snails

Slugs are one of the most persistent garden pests, and few people can eradicate them entirely from their garden. It helps to attract wildlife such as hedgehogs, slow worms, frogs and toads which eat slugs (see Wildlife gardening, page 124), but with or without these you'll still have a battle on your hands. Here are the best tactics:

o There is a biological control for slugs – nematodes – which doesn't control snails. The nematodes tend to kill the young and smaller slugs in the soil rather than larger ones on the surface.

o You can buy slug and snail traps, or just use a plastic tub or jar. Bury it in the ground until it's almost level with the surface of the soil, and half fill it with beer. The slugs are attracted by the beer and fall in and drown. The downside of this method is that other insects also fall in, especially ground beetles which are your friends. I've even known a newt drown in a slug trap (perhaps that's the origin of the expression 'as pissed as a newt').

o Copper gives slugs and snails a shock, and keeps them away. You can buy copper rings to go round plants, copper tape to stick round the rim of flower pots, and copper coated mats to put under pots or cut to fit where you need it.

o Sharp gravel around your plants helps deter slugs, too.

o Hunt slugs or snails at night when they're at their most active, especially in wet weather. Take a torch and never mind what the neighbours think. If you don't enjoy killing them, put them in a bucket of salty water or paraffin. Don't release them nearby: they'll be back.

o Slugs and snails need daytime hiding places so you can set traps by leaving half grapefruits turned down on the soil, a plank of wood or a bit of old carpet. Go round during the day and catch your slugs and snails by turning over the traps.

↬ Common pests and how to control them

Here are some of the most common garden pests and why you don't want them, along with how to get rid of them.

Damage	Control
Aphids, Caterpillars (particularly cabbage white), Sawfly, Thrips	
Aphids suck sap from stems and flowers and transfer viruses from plant to plant. Caterpillars eat leaves of plants and sometimes flowers. Thrips eat leaves, giving them a silvery appearance. Sawfly larvae eat and burrow into fruit, vegetables and flowers.	Spray with Derris or use the biological control *bacillus thuringiensis* which you buy in powder form and add to water.
Blackfly, Greenfly	
Suck out sap from stems, leaves and fruit.	Spray with soapy liquid, or encourage ladybirds, hoverfly larvae and lacewing larvae to control them. You can buy ladybird and lacewing larvae from April to August from good organic garden suppliers.

Damage	Control
Chafer grubs, Leather jackets, Vine weevil larvae	
Chafer grubs eat roots of herbaceous plants, fruit and vegetables. Leather jackets feed on roots, especially of grass. Vine weevils feed on leaves and the larvae damage roots.	Nematodes are the biological pest control to use here. Otherwise it's a matter of killing them by hand if and when you find them.
Earwig	
Eat flower buds, flower heads and leaves.	They feed at night and need somewhere to hide by day. Put straw filled plant pots upside down on top of sticks/stakes near where the earwigs are feeding. They will crawl up the stick and, during the day, you can shake them out of the straw into a bucket of water.
Red spider mite	
Suck sap from foliage.	They like dry conditions, so drench with cold water. Or spray with insecticidal soap (an organic soap compound) and/or use the biological control *phytoseiulus*, a tiny predatory mite which feeds on them.

Damage	Control
Whitefly	
Eat the underside of leaves which can then develop moulds.	Spray with insecticidal soap and/or use the biological control *encarsia*, which is a tiny parasitic wasp.
Wireworm	
The larvae of click beetle, these feed on roots and underground parts of many plants.	Dig over the ground thoroughly and then weed. Birds love them so the aim is to bring them to the surface and then clear the weeds so the birds can get at them.

Other garden pests and vermin such as mice, rats, rabbits and squirrels can be trapped, as can birds such as magpies, rooks and crows. Agricultural suppliers (among others) sell traps which capture the animals humanely if you prefer, and they can be released a good distance away – at least a quarter of a mile and up to two miles for larger birds. Try not to release them where they'll plague some other poor gardener (though if you have any enemies living a mile or two away who are keen gardeners…).

You can also keep rabbits out by removing their access to the garden. Block any areas which aren't walled with wire netting, preferably with the foot of it sunk into the ground (rabbits can burrow, after all). If this doesn't work (and I can't guarantee it will) you can try a strand of electric wire just above the ground around your vegetable garden.

The best way to keep pigeons and other birds off your soft

fruit is by growing the fruit inside a cage. You can drape netting over the fruit but birds can easily get trapped in loose netting and strangle themselves.

Pocket facts

If you're stung by a *bee* while gardening, apply a solution of bicarbonate of soda which should help neutralise the sting since bee stings are acid.

Wasp and *hornet* stings, on the other hand, are alkaline so you should treat them with an acid such as lemon juice or vinegar.

Apparently Eau de Cologne, should you happen to have any, eases the pain of ant bites, though I haven't yet had a chance to test this (nor am I seeking an opportunity to do so).

Hairy *caterpillars* can irritate the skin if the hairs get left in it. Apply vinegar to relieve the rash.

For *nettle* stings, crush a dock leaf in your hand and press it against the rash.

If you get a strong allergic reaction to any insect or plant bite or sting, get medical help.

⤳ Plants to deter pests

The best way of all to deter pests from ever getting a hold is to grow plants which attract their natural predators. Here are some plants you can try to make room for in your garden to help control some of the worst pests.

Plant	Beneficial wildlife attracted	Which deters...
Alyssum	Hoverfly, ladybird	Aphids
Catnip	Hoverfly	Aphids
Celery	Beneficial wasps	Aphids, caterpillars
Dill	Hoverfly, lacewing, ladybird, parasitic wasps	Aphids, caterpillars, leafhoppers, mealy bugs, mites, whitefly
Feverfew	Hoverfly	Aphids
Lavender	Hoverfly	Aphids
Mint	Hoverflies, beneficial wasps and others	Aphids, caterpillars
Penstemon	Hoverfly, ladybird	Aphids
Poached egg plant	Hoverfly	Aphids
Sedum	Hoverfly	Aphids
Sunflower	Lacewing, beneficial wasps	Aphids, caterpillars, leafhoppers, mealy bugs, mites
Thyme	Hoverfly	Aphids
Veronica	Hoverfly, ladybird	Aphids
Yarrow	Hoverfly, ladybird, parasitic wasps	Aphids, whitefly

See also natural pest control in the Wildlife gardening section, on page 137.

∾ Diseases ∾

There are scores of diseases which affect specific plants such as celery heart rot, hollyhock rust or peach leaf curl. There isn't room to list them all here and if you think your plant is suffering from its own personal disease, best look it up in a specialist book. However there are some diseases which are quite widespread and may affect many of your plants.

If you think what you're looking at is a common disease, here's a quick guide to check what to do about it.

Disease	Appearance	Treatment
Black spot	Attacks *roses*. Dark brown spots on foliage and stems.	Spray with garlic solution or grow *garlic* nearby. Or grow resistant varieties.
Canker	Attacks fruit trees, especially *apples*. Sunken area on the bark near a bud.	Cut out the diseased area and burn the wood. Clean the wound. Paint with a fungicidal wound paint.
Mildew	Fungal threads that suck the sap. Often appears as a silvery white powder coating leaves and stems.	Hard to control but healthy plants are less likely to suffer. Feed and water. Burn affected plants if they don't recover.

Disease	Appearance	Treatment
Rust	Yellow, brown or orange spots on leaves.	Many different fungi attack garden plants and need different treatments. Try to collect and burn all affected leaves, and grow the plant in a different part of the garden next year.
Wilt	Not really a disease but a symptom caused by various fungi.	Most plants need to be dug up and burnt, but *clematis* often recover and, if left undisturbed, reshoot later in the year or even the following year.

Appendix I
Monthly jobs

There's always plenty to do in even the smallest garden. The question, at any given time, is what? You don't want to realise in April that you forgot to prune your roses in February and it's now too late. So before you go indoors, have a quick run through the vital jobs for this month and make sure you haven't missed anything.

∾ January ∾

o Dig over heavy soil when the weather allows, incorporating compost or manure to improve the texture of the soil. Leave it rough for now and don't dig in any manure yet.

o Turn the compost heap.

o Find the places where snails are overwintering such as walls and leaf litter, and destroy them.

o Cover soil with fleece or cloches to warm it up if you plan to sow early crops.

o Watch out for storm damage to trees and shrubs. Remove any damaged branches and prune them with a clean cut.

o Plant deciduous hedges and bare rooted trees and shrubs.

o Plant roses if the soil is not too wet or cold.

o Start forcing *rhubarb*.

o Clean out the garden shed (well, it probably needs doing and now's the best time. At least you'll be out of the worst of the weather in there).

∾ February ∾

o Cut back ivy on walls before the birds start nesting. Be ruthless – it grows back amazingly quickly.

o Prune greenhouse climbers.

o This is the month to sort out *wisteria* if you grow it: cut back to one or two buds from the main stem, removing whippy growth except where you need to train new leaders.

o Finish planting (and, if relevant, laying) deciduous hedges and bare rooted trees and shrubs.

o Sow *parsley* if the weather is dry and not too cold.

o Start sowing *sweet peas* and half-hardy annuals inside.

o Chit seed *potatoes*.

o Cut back late flowering *clematis* at the end of the month.

∾ March ∾

o Tidy flower borders, cutting back old growth, and top dress with compost.

o Divide overgrown perennials.

o In mild weather, give the lawn its first cut, with the mower on a high setting.

o Prune *roses*.

o Sow hardy annuals outside.

o Begin successional planting of hardy leaf and root vegetables.

o Sow *leek*, early *beetroot*, *peas*, *lettuce*, *onion sets* and *shallots* outside.

o Sow *tomato*, *sweet pepper*, *squash* and *courgette* seeds inside.

o Plant early *potatoes* at the end of the month.

∾ April ∾

o Plant late flowering herbaceous plants.

o Plant out the *sweet pea* seedlings you sowed in February.

o Move young plants from the greenhouse to the cold frame to harden off.

o Shorten straggly shoots on *camellias* after flowering.

o Prepare your *runner bean* beds.

o Sow *broccoli* seed, *kale*, *spinach beet*, *cauliflower* and *winter cabbage* outside.

o Pick off bright red lily beetles from *lilies* and *fritillaries* and squash them.

o April is a good month to plant a *lavender* hedge.

∾ May ∾

o Clear pots and containers for summer plants. (Bulbs can be moved into a trench in the garden. They will happily die back ready for planting in the autumn.)

o Pinch out shoots on *grapevines*.

o Take softwood cuttings of herbs.

o Harden off indoor grown plants ready for planting out.

o Tie in greenhouse *tomatoes*.

o Earth up potatoes if frosts are likely and the shoots are above ground. If frost has specifically been forecast cover them with newspaper.

o Sow *runner beans*, main crop *beetroot*, *basil* and *marjoram* outside.

o Hoe weeds in the vegetable garden regularly, and water it when dry.

June

o Cut back early flowering shrubs after flowering.

o Cut back early flowering herbaceous plants after flowering to 2-3" from the ground to encourage fresh growth such as *alyssum saxatile*, *aubretia*.

o Divide *primroses* and *polyanthus* for replanting.

o Sow *wallflower*, *viola*, *foxglove*, *Canterbury bell* and *sweet William* for flowering next year.

o Transplant sprouting *broccoli*, *Brussels sprout*, summer *cabbage*, *cauliflower*, *kale* and *leek* to final positions.

o Plant out *aubergine*, *tomato*, *pepper*, *squash*, *courgette*.

o Pinch out growing tips of *runner beans* when they reach the top of their support.

o Tie in *tomatoes* as they grow.

o Remove flowering shoots on *rhubarb*.

∾ July ∾

o Water new lawns if the weather is dry.

o Cut spring wild flower meadows and remove the grass.

o Cut back whippy growths on wisteria.

o Deadhead *roses, peonies, pansies* etc.

o Cut back early flowering herbaceous plants when they've finished flowering.

o Take half-ripe cuttings of shrubs such as *cistus, lavatera, viburnum*.

o Continue pinching out growing tips of *runner beans*.

o Thin *apple* and *pear* crops if the fruit is too prolific.

o Once *strawberries* have finished fruiting, remove old foliage (and straw if you've used it).

∾ August ∾

o Prune rambling *roses* when they've finished flowering.

o Continue deadheading herbaceous plants and cut off tall, weak stems.

o Plant out well grown perennial seedlings in nursery beds.

o Plant *daffodil* bulbs to flower next spring.

o Take *lavender, sage* and *perennial wallflower* cuttings.

o Take cuttings of shrubs, *heather, geranium (pelargonium), fuchsia* and *hydrangea*.

o Bend over the tops of *onions* as they ripen.

o Sow varieties of *onions* which will mature from late June-July next year.

o Sow spring *lettuce, winter spinach*, late *carrots*.

o Summer prune restricted forms of *apple* and *pear* trees (such as espalier or fan trained).

∾ September ∾

o This is a good month for sowing grass seed.

o On a warm day clear the unheated greenhouse and wash it down with mild disinfectant to maximise winter light and deter pests and diseases.

o Remove dying annuals to make room for spring bedding and bulbs.

o Clip hedges for the last time this season.

o Take *rose* cuttings.

o Plant bulbs in flower beds and containers (except for *tulips*).

o Plant prepared bulbs, such as *hyacinth*, for indoor flowering.

o Clear away any crops that have finished producing eg stumps of *cabbages* or *peas*.

o Sow *parsley* for a spring crop.

o Plant *garlic*.

o Pick fruit as it ripens.

o Harvest all remaining crops that may be susceptible to frost, eg *marrow, pumpkin, squash*, maincrop *potatoes*.

o Cut down *asparagus* foliage at the end of the month (if you were intrepid and clever enough to grow it in the first place).

∾ October ∾

o A good month for laying turf·or sowing grass seed.

o Rake up leaves.

o Cover ponds with netting to prevent leaves falling in.

o Remove all saucers under pots to prevent frost damage to them.

o Tie in new growth on climbers to prevent damage in high winds.

o Transplant self-sown *forget-me-nots* to where you want them.

o Plant herbaceous plants now to give them a good chance to settle in before winter.

o Plant out biennials such as *wallflower, foxglove, Canterbury bell, viola, sweet William*.

o Start planting *tulip* bulbs.

o Plant out hardy perennials sown from seed once they're large enough.

o Lift *dahlia* tubers in cold areas.

o Plant *rhubarb* crowns.

o Continue harvesting autumn fruit.

o Examine all stored crops regularly.

∼ November ∼

o This may be your last chance to save any half hardy plants you've left outside.

o Clean out bird nesting boxes.

o Rake up leaves and stack in wire netting or in a black plastic sack for future leaf mould. You can add leaf mould accelerator to speed the process.

o Remove netting from the pond as soon as the leaves have fallen to prevent birds and other wildlife becoming tangled in it.

o Remove dead foliage from *hostas* to deter slugs.

o Cut back the growth on well established *roses* by half to prevent wind rock.

o Plant *roses*.

o Finish planting *tulips*.

o Plant new soft fruit canes eg *raspberries, loganberries*.

o Sow earliest varieties of *broad beans*, eg 'Aquadulce', 'Jade'.

o Continue to check stored fruit and vegetables.

o Start planting bare rooted hedging, trees and shrubs at the end of the month.

∼ December ∼

o Dig over areas of the lawn that will need to be reseeded in the spring.

o Clean and repair tools and wash pots and seed trays.

o Lag outdoor water taps and pipes.

o Keep an area of the pond ice free if possible by covering it with boards, or float a large soft beachball on it (if you don't mind reliving *The Prisoner*).

o Tidy herbaceous borders.

o Remove dead foliage from around roses to help control blackspot (and do not compost).

o Check stakes and ties and replace where necessary.

o Winter prune free standing *apple, pear* and *quince* trees.

Appendix II
Plant names

As I mentioned in the introduction, I've been inconsistent in my use of Latin and English names for plants, using whatever name seems to be the most common. So here are two lists (one English-Latin, the other Latin-English) where you can look up any plant name I've used elsewhere in the book and find the alternative name for it.

∼ English/Latin ∼

Aconite	eranthis hyemalis
African marigold	tagetes erecta
Autumn crocus	colchicum autumnale
Autumn cyclamen	cyclamen neapolitanum/hederafolium
Autumn gentian	gentiana sino-ornata
Daisy	bellis
Barberry	berberis
Black-eyed Susan	thunbergia alata
Borage	borago
Buttercup	ranunculus
Bow Bells	camellia williamsii
Canterbury bells	campanula medium
Carnation	dianthus
Catmint	nepeta
Catnip	nepeta
Chickweed	stellaria
Chicory	cichorium

Chocolate cosmos	cosmos atrosanguineus
Christmas rose	helleborus niger
Cineraria	senecio cineraria
Clover	trifolium
Columbine	aquilegia
Common broom	cytisus scoparius
Common gorse	ulex europaeus
Cornflower	centaurea cyanus
Cotton lavender	santolina chamaecyparissus
Cowslip	primula veris
Crab apple	malus
Cuckoo flower	cardamine pratensis
Daffodil	narcissus
Dandelion	crepis
Dock	rumex
Double daisy	bellis perennis
Elder	sambucus
Evening primrose	oenothera
Feverfew	tanacetum parthenium
Flax	linum
Flowering currant	ribes sanguineum
Forget-me-not	myosotis
Foxglove	digitalis
French lavender	lavandula dentata/lavandula stoechus
Gentian	gentiana
Goldenrod	solidago
Ground elder	aegopodium
Groundsel	senecio vulgaris
Heather	erica
Hellebore	helleborus
Heuchera	alum root
Hollyhock	alcea
Honesty	lunaria

Honeysuckle	lonicera
Hyacinth	hyacinthus
Hybrid tea rose	rosa x
Hyssop	hyssopus
Japanese anemone	anemone x hybrida
Japonica	chaenomeles
Jasmine	jasminum
Kaffir lily	schizostylis
Knapweed	centaurea
Lady's mantle	alchemilla
Lady's smock	cardamine pratensis
Larkspur	consolida
Lavender	lavandula
Lemon verbena	aloysia triphylla
Lilac	syringa
Love-in-a-mist	nigella damascena
Lupin	lupinus
Madonna lily	lilium candidum
Marigold	calendula/tagetes
Martagon lily	lilium martagon
Michaelmas daisy	aster
Mistletoe	viscum album
Morning glory	ipomoea hederacea
Nasturtium	tropaeolum
Night-scented stock	matthiola bicornis
Oleander	nerium oleander
Opium poppy	papaver somniferum
Oriental hellebore	helleborus orientalis
Oriental poppy	papaver orientale
Ox-eye daisy	leucanthemum vulgare
Pansy	viola wittrockiana
Pasque flower	pulsatilla vulgaris
Passion flower	passiflora

Pelargonium	geranium
Peony	paeonia
Perennial wallflower	erysimum
Periwinkle	vinca
Pineapple sage	salvia rutilans
Plantain	plantago
Poached egg plant	limnanthes douglasii
Poppy	papaver
Pot marigold	calendula officinalis
Primrose	primula vulgaris
Regal lily	lilium regale
Rosemary	rosmarinus officinalis
Russian vine	polygonum aubertii
Salad burnet	sanguisorba minor
Saxifrage	saxifraga
Scabious	scabiosa
Scarlet flax	linum rubrum
Scarlet pimpernel	anagallis arvensis
Snapdragon	antirrhinum
Snowdrop	galanthus
Sunflower	helianthus
Sweet bergamot	monarda
Sweet pea	lathyrus odoratus
Sweet William	dianthus barbatus
Teasel	dipsacus fullonum
Thistle	carlina
Toad lily	tricyrtis
Tobacco plant	nicotiana
Tulip	tulipa
Valerian	valeriana
Violet	viola
Virginia creeper	parthenocissus quinquefolia
White campion	silene latifolia alba
Winter heliotrope	petasites fragrans

Winter iris	iris unguicularis
Winter jasmine	jasminum nudiflorum
Wintersweet	chimonanthus
Witch hazel	hamamelis
Yarrow	achillea millefolium

～ Latin/English ～

Many of the plants commonly referred to by their Latin names don't really have an English name so there's not much point my trying to list it. Here, however, are the Latin plant names I've used which *do* have a common English name.

Actinidia kolomikta	kolomikta vine
Ageratum	floss flower
Anagallis arvensis	scarlet pimpernel
Aquilegia	columbine
Argyranthemum	marguerite
Aster	Michaelmas daisy
Bellis	daisy
Bellis perennis	double daisy
Berberis	barberry
Camellia willliamsii	Bow Bells
Chionodoxa	glory of the snow
Cistus	rock rose
Cleome spinosa	spider flower
Colchicum autumnale	autumn crocus
Cornus	dogwood
Cyclamen neopolitanum	autumn cyclamen
Datura brugmansia	angels' trumpet
Doronicum	leopard's bane
Hosta	funkia/plantain lily
Lavatera	tree mallow

Linaria	toadflax
Meconopsis	blue poppy
Nepeta	catmint/catnip
Prunus subhirtella	higan cherry/winter flowering cherry
Pyracanthus	firethorn
Romneya	Californian poppy
Rudbeckia	coneflower
Sambucus	elder
Schizanthus	butterfly flower/poor man's orchid
Sedum	stonecrop
Viola	violet

∾ Contact us ∾

You're welcome to contact White Ladder Press if you have any questions or comments for either us or the author. Please use whichever of the following routes suits you.

Phone: 01803 813343

Email: enquiries@whiteladderpress.com

Fax: 01803 813928

Address: White Ladder Press, Great Ambrook, Near Ipplepen, Devon TQ12 5UL

Website: www.whiteladderpress.com

∾ What can our website do for you? ∾

If you want more information about any of our books, you'll find it at **www.whiteladderpress.com**. In particular you'll find extracts from each of our books, and reviews of those that are already published. We also run special offers on future titles if you order online before publication. And you can request a copy of our free catalogue.

Many of our books also have links pages, useful addresses and so on relevant to the subject of the book. You can find out a bit more about us and, if you're a writer yourself, you'll find our submission guidelines for authors. So please check us out and let us know if you have any comments, questions or suggestions.

∾ Fancy another good read? ∾

If you've enjoyed this book, how about reading another of our books? *Recipes for Disasters How to turn kitchen cock-ups into magnificent meals*, also by Roni Jay, will help you ensure that every meal you serve up looks perfect, whatever may have gone on behind the scenes.

So the pastry has burnt, the pudding has collapsed or the terrine won't turn out. Or the main ingredient has been eaten by the cat. Or perhaps it's the guests who've buggered everything up: they forgot to mention that they're vegetarian (you've made a beef bourgignon). Or they've brought along a friend (you've only made six crème brulées).

But don't panic. There are few kitchen cock-ups that can't be successfully salvaged if you know how. With the right attitude you are no longer accident-prone, but adaptable. Not a panicker but a creative, inspirational cook. *Recipes for Disasters* is packed with useful tips and ideas for making sure that your entertaining always runs smoothly (or at least appears to). Yes, you still can have a reputation as a culinary paragon, even if it is all bluff.

On the next few pages is a taster of what you'll find in *Recipes for Disasters*. If you like the look of it and want to order a copy you can call us on 01803 813343 or order online at **www.whiteladderpress.com**.

Recipes for Disasters

The timing goes all wrong

I was cooking a meal which I was really pleased with, right up to the last minute. The meat was cooked, the potatoes and runner beans dished up, the sauce ready... but the damn broccoli wouldn't cook. By the time it was ready everything else was either getting cold out of the oven or going dry in it. I was so upset.

Disappointed from Devon

It's always the bloody broccoli in my experience. That's because I steam it; it cooks much faster, of course, if you put it straight in the water. Actually, getting everything ready at the same time is arguably the toughest part of cooking for guests. There are things you can do when it happens, but long term it's also worth knowing how to minimise the risk of it happening at all.

Cure

If you find yourself with half the meal ready to go and the other half not yet cooked, it doesn't help to be told how you might have prevented it if you'd thought ahead. So here are some tips that might help if you're in trouble:

o Put anything you can in a low oven to keep warm. Put butter on vegetables, and a lid or cover over them, to prevent them drying out.

o Speed up the offending item of food in some way. For example, take the broccoli off the stove, cut the stems off, and put it back on to cook quicker. Or take it out of the steamer and put it into a pan of boiling water (the one at the bottom of the steamer will do nicely). Or cut up meat into smaller pieces.

o Abandon the thing. This doesn't work for the main dish, but you might be able to give up on one vegetable and never mention that you'd planned to serve it.

o Wait. Maybe it doesn't matter that much if you're more flexible about the timing. Just delay the start of the meal. If the pudding is cooking slower than you thought just take a longer break between courses. Lots of people do it anyway; just let your guests think you're the kind of people who go in for long, relaxed meals.

o If things get a bit cold, you can often disguise it by making sure you serve any sauce or gravy piping hot.

o If the meal is delayed, find something to serve as a pre-meal snack — a bag of Bombay mix or a packet of crisps (see page 00). Not only does it keep people happy, it also gives the impression that you always meant to serve the meal later.

Prevention

If you have a persistent problem with timing (and lots of us do) there are ways to minimise the risk. Even if you want to learn to perfect the timing thing, at least you can take these preventative measures for the occasional meal that you really want to get right.

o Steam your vegetables. The point of this is that if something else slows you down you can keep the vegetable water simmering lightly in the steamer and the vegetables won't lose their flavour or their colour in the way they would if you overcooked them in water.

o ...apart from broccoli. I'm very fond of the stuff, but it does seem to be one of the most frequent culprits when timing goes wrong. It's fine if you cook it in boiling water, but if you steam it, it somehow always takes longer than you could possibly expect.

o Serve salad instead of vegetables.

o Cook what you can in advance so it has only to heat through and not actually cook from scratch.

o If you're cooking anything that won't overcook, put it in early so it can't *undercook*, leaving you juggling the rest of the meal while you wait for it. In other words if you're cooking, say, Moroccan braised lamb shank which is supposed to take three hours, you know perfectly well that it will taste even better after four hours. So put it in four hours before you eat and you can be even more confident that it will be ready on time.

Salvage secrets

Just because you knew when you invited your guests for 8pm that you planned to eat at 8.30, it doesn't mean they know it. If things go wrong, just give yourself more time. Eat at 9pm instead – they won't know any different. The same applies to how long a break you take between courses.

Index